PALEY

PALEY

Evidences for the Man

M. L. CLARKE

UNIVERSITY OF TORONTO
PRESS

First published 1974
by the S.P.C.K., London

© M. L. Clarke 1974

First published 1974 in Canada and
the United States of America
by University of Toronto Press
Toronto and Buffalo

Printed in Great Britain
ISBN 0–8020–2112–3
LC 73–86991

Contents

Preface

'No modern writer perhaps has diffused more widely the knowledge of moral and religious truth. None has seen his works pass through more editions in the same time: and none will be found with more certainty to hold a place on the shelf of every private library.' So the *Quarterly Review* wrote of Paley in 1809, four years after his death, and in the next year William Windham asserted in the House of Commons that Paley's works 'had done more for the moral improvement of mankind than perhaps the writing of any other man that had ever existed'. His reputation did not remain at this high level, but his works continued to be read, the last complete edition appearing in 1877; and there must be Cambridge men still alive for whom 'Paley' recalls memories of 'Little Go', an examination for which Paley's *Evidences of Christianity* remained on the syllabus until as late as 1920. His writings are not marked by any great profundity or originality, but they are written in a clear and vigorous style and can still be read with pleasure and profit. Their real merits, combined with the author's engaging personality, justify, I hope, a new study of this once famous writer.

Paley's writings were not closely related to the events of his life and I have therefore thought it best to treat his life and his works separately. He himself observed that his works should be read in the reverse order to that of composition; logically *Natural Theology* should come first, followed by *Evidences* (revealed religion), with *Moral and Political Philosophy* last. The order in which I have handled them is a mixture of the chronological and the logical; it seemed natural to deal with his earliest work first, and after that I have deserted chronology and discussed the rest of his work in what might be considered the logical order of its subject matter.

The main sources for Paley's life are the biographies of G. M. Meadley and Edmund Paley. Meadley's *Memoirs of the Life of William Paley* was first published in 1809; a second, enlarged, edition appeared in 1810. Edmund Paley's life of his father formed the first volume of his edition of Paley's works published in 1825, and was reprinted in the

1838 edition. Meadley was primarily interested in Paley as one of those Friends of Civil and Religious Liberty, of Private Happiness and of Public Virtue to whom he dedicated his book. Edmund Paley on the other hand was concerned to show his father as he was in the home and the parish; what was new in his work, he wrote, was 'derived from family recollections and the domestic life of an affectionate father'. Apart from these two works the only source worth special mention is H. D. Best's *Literary and Personal Memorials*, which includes some lively anecdotes of Paley as the writer knew him in his last years at Lincoln.

The most complete edition of Paley's works is that of Edmund Paley, which includes a number of sermons additional to those previously published. In view, however, of the large number of editions both of the collected works and of individual books, it would be no help to the reader to give page references to a particular one, which might not be available to him, and I have therefore given references by title and chapter number. References to the sermons are to the numbering in Edmund Paley's edition, but I have added in brackets the number as given in other editions.

Since the text was completed I have seen, through the kindness of Mr D. F. R. Missen, a xerox copy of a manuscript book, preserved at Christ's College, Cambridge, containing extracts from Paley's divinity lectures and some notes of his Greek Testament lectures. The MS contains nothing of importance not already published.

I am grateful to all those who have provided me with information or helped me in other ways.

In addition to those whose help is acknowledged in the notes my thanks are due to Miss Mary Cotterell, Mr C. R. Davey, Mr Warren Derry, Mr D. F. R. Missen, Dr A. N. L. Munby, and Dr A. L. Peck.

Abbreviations

The following abbreviations have been used in the notes:

PALEY'S WORKS

M. and P.P.: *Principles of Moral and Political Philosophy*

Evidences: *A View of the Evidences of Christianity*

N.T.: *Natural Theology*

BIOGRAPHICAL SOURCES

M.: G. M. Meadley, *Memoirs of the Life of William Paley*, 2nd edn (Edinburgh 1810)

E.P.: Paley's *Works*, edited by Edmund Paley, 2nd edn (1838), Vol. I

Best: H. D. Best, *Literary and Personal Memorials* (1829)

✳ 1 ✳
Early Life

In the parish of Giggleswick in the West Riding of Yorkshire there are two farms known as High and Low Paley Green. From these, it is believed, the Paley family originated and drew its name.[1] In the village of Langcliffe, a short distance from Giggleswick and formerly in its parish, the house still stands which belonged to the family until recently, though they had long ceased to live there.[2] Inside it is a beam with the initials H.P. and the date 1676, but the front of the house with its mullioned windows is evidently of earlier date. This modest house, that of a yeoman rather than a country gentleman, was the birthplace of Paley's father.

Paley, who was without social pretensions and liked to emphasize the humble connections of his family, would recall a great-uncle who kept a hardware stall in the market of Settle, the nearby town which was originally in Giggleswick parish, and another kinsman who kept a grocer's shop there.[3] He was fond of telling the story of his coat of arms. 'When I set up a carriage, it was thought that my armorial bearings should appear on the panels. Now, we had none of us ever heard of the Paley arms; none of us ever dreamed that such things existed or had ever been. All the old folks of the family were consulted; they knew nothing about it. Great search was made, however, and at last we found a silver tankard, on which was engraved a coat of arms. It was carried by common consent that these *must* be the Paley arms; they were painted on the carriage and looked very handsome. The carriage went on very well with them; and it was not till six months afterwards that we found out that the tankard had been bought at a sale.'[4] Paley's son maintains that he was indulging in what would today be called inverted snobbery and that the tankard had in fact originally belonged to the branch of the family which owned the property at Langcliffe.[5] Whether this is the case or not, Paley would no doubt be amused to know that the Paleys of Langcliffe, complete with coat of arms, have found a place in Burke's *Landed Gentry*.

For younger sons the grammar school at Giggleswick opened the way to the universities and the learned professions, and as early as the seventeenth century Paleys are found at Christ's College, Cambridge, where eight scholarships for boys from Giggleswick school were founded in 1616. Paley's father, second son of Thomas Paley of Langcliffe, proceeded to Christ's, took his degree in 1733, and became vicar of Helpstone near Peterborough and Minor Canon of the cathedral. In 1745, however, he returned to his native parish to become master of Giggleswick school, a post which he held for forty-four years until his death in 1799 at the age of eighty-eight. He was a cheerful, witty man, fond of company, but at the same time very much the schoolmaster. 'When at the age of eighty-three or eighty-four he was obliged to have assistance ... he used to be wheeled in his chair to his school, and even in the delirium of his last illness insisted upon giving his daughters a Greek author, over which they would mutter and mumble, to persuade him that he was still teaching his boys Greek.' He was inclined to be irritable and carried into the home the exercise of authority to which he was used in school. 'He was found in the hay-field among his work people or sitting in his elbow chair nibbling his stick, or with the tail of his damask gown rolled into his pocket busying himself in his garden even at the age of eighty; and if he could not improve it, was not seldom detected in making a common destruction of walk, border and grassplot.'[6]

In 1742 he married Elizabeth Clapham, of Stackhouse, a hamlet less than a mile from Langcliffe on the other side of the Ribble valley. She brought with her a dowry of £400 and was thought to have married beneath her. She was 'a little shrewd-looking keen-eyed woman, of remarkable strength of mind and spirits; one of those positive characters that decide promptly and execute at once; of a sanguine and irritable temper which led her to be constantly on the alert in thinking and acting'; a good manager, who insisted on her servants rising at 4 o'clock, and if they overslept cured them of the habit by taking up their breakfast and with a curtsey 'presenting it to the ladies'.[7]

Their son William, who retained throughout life a pronounced north-country accent,[8] was not a Yorkshireman by birth. He was born at Peterborough in July 1743, but two years later moved with his parents to Giggleswick, travelling on his mother's lap as she rode on horseback behind her husband, with all their worldly goods in a tea-chest.[9] He was at school under his father. Giggleswick school was then housed in a 'low small and irregular building',[10] but it had a good reputation among the northern grammar schools, and Paley was well grounded in the classics there. He was a tall, ungainly, talkative boy, guileless and good-natured, with no taste for ordinary sports, but fond of fishing, to which he remained addicted, despite his scanty success, throughout his life. He had an insatiable curiosity. He would question old women knitting or joiners at work; he once sat up all night watching the process of soap boiling and on another occasion he was found pulling out a girl's tooth in imitation of a quack doctor whom he had seen performing the operation. He showed an early interest in the law which remained with him in adult life; after visiting the assizes at Lancaster he arranged a mock trial at school at which he presided as Judge.

At the age of fifteen, in November 1758, he was taken by his father to Cambridge to be admitted to Christ's. He was never a good horseman, and riding on his pony behind his father, he fell off seven times. 'I was lighter then', he would say when telling the story, 'than I am now, and my falls were not likely to be serious, so that I soon began to care little about them. My father, though at first a good deal alarmed at my awkwardness, afterwards became so accustomed to it, that he would only turn his head half aside and say, "Get up, and take care of thy money, lad".'[11] He did not go into residence till the following year, and the intervening time was spent with a private tutor in mathematics, one William Howarth of Ditchford near Ripon. He spent much of his time alone, wandering about and musing, and his awkward ill-directed movements gave him the reputation of being a bit crazed. He attended the assizes at York when Eugene Aram, the subject of a once well-known poem by Hood, was tried and condemned for murder. In later life, defending the inclusion of Aram in a biographical dictionary, he said: 'Nay, a man that has been hanged has some pretension to notoriety; and especially a man who has got himself hanged by his own cleverness, which Eugene Aram certainly did.'[12]

Paley was sixteen when he went up to Cambridge in 1759. 'I was sent,' he used to say, 'earlier to Cambridge than any young man before or since; and the reason was this—my mother wished to make a baker of me, and my father had made up his mind that I should be a parson.'[13] He was wrong in saying that he went up earlier than anyone before or since. The usual age of entry to the English universities had originally been about fourteen, and though it had risen to eighteen by Paley's day, boys still occasionally went up at fifteen or sixteen. But most of his fellow freshmen would be two years or more older than he, and he always maintained that it had been a mistake to send him to Cambridge so young. He entered Christ's as a sizar, but at the end of his first term exchanged this status for that of a scholar. The fees of sizars were lower than those of pensioners, and when Paley went into residence, there were still colleges at which they had to perform menial tasks like waiting in hall.[14] But the social stigma which consequently attached to a sizarship can hardly have existed at Christ's; of the ten admitted as sizars in 1758 all became scholars in the course of their first year of residence, and since seven of the nine pensioners similarly succeeded to scholarships virtually all the undergraduates had the same status.[15]

Paley's mathematical training gave him an advantage over his fellow undergraduates, most of whom came up completely ignorant of what was to be their chief study at Cambridge. In classics, since he had left the grammar school at fifteen, he was not so well equipped. He was generally held to be deficient in classical learning,[16] and when in later life he had to deliver a Latin sermon before the university he committed the unforgivable sin of perpetrating a false quantity, *profūgus* for *profŭgus*. His blunder was perpetuated in a feeble epigram:

> *Italiam fato profugus Lavinaque venit*
> *Litora.*
> *Errat Vergilius; forte profugus erat.*

Richard Watson, who like Paley was the son of a north-country schoolmaster and like him left school early, recalls the trouble he had over Latin quantities and the resentment he felt at the time spent on the acquisition of this worthless knowledge.[17] Paley would not have worried or cared much if he had made a mistake. His Latin and Greek were in fact adequate for his needs, and though he had no interest in classical scholarship for its own sake and never paraded his knowledge, he continued to read Virgil, Horace, and Cicero for pleasure throughout his life.[18] He learned easily, but had no desire to pursue learning beyond his immediate needs. His great asset was his clarity of mind. When he had left for Cambridge his father remarked: 'He'll turn out a great man—very great indeed—I'm certain of it; for he has by far the clearest head I ever met with in my life.'[19]

'There is no university, I believe, in Europe,' wrote Bishop Watson, 'where the degree of Batchelor of Arts is more honourably obtained than in the University of Cambridge; the sedulity with which the young men, in general, pursue the plan of studying which is prescribed for them is highly commendable.'[20] Certainly Cambridge of the eighteenth century compares favourably with contemporary Oxford. Oxford was conservative, Cambridge progressive; Oxford remained faithful to Aristotle, Cambridge followed Locke and Newton. At Oxford the degree examinations had become a mere formality, at Cambridge they were taken seriously and conducted fairly. There were, however, weaknesses in the Cambridge system. The range of subjects studied was narrow, being virtually confined to mathematics and natural philosophy, with a little metaphysics and moral philosophy; and apart from a few professorial lectures, teaching was in the hands of college tutors who were not always men of the highest calibre. Moreover, the student body included a number of Noblemen and Fellow Commoners who could take their degrees without examination. These and other wealthy and idle young men, for whom the university provided an agreeable scene for the pursuit of pleasure, could lead the more studious into bad ways. Bishop Watson describes how, returning to his rooms after a party at one or two in the morning, he would see a light in the rooms of one of those who like himself had come to the university to work, and would be inspired by his example to spend the next day in hard study. Henry Gunning, after spending the day with his agreeable but idle friends, would be kept awake by remorse for a large part of the night.[21]

When Gunning was at Christ's in the seventeen-eighties, one of the tutors lectured on classics, in addition to moral philosophy and logic.[22] There is no record of Paley's having to attend classical lectures. When he was an undergraduate one of the tutors, Anthony Shepherd, lectured on algebra, geometry, and natural philosophy, the other, William Backhouse, on logic, metaphysics, and moral philosophy. Paley was excused from attending Shepherd's college lectures, presumably because they were too elementary, though he was required to go to those he gave as Plumian professor, and in his third year he went to what the Victorians called a coach, John Wilson of Peterhouse, afterwards a successful lawyer and a close friend of Paley.[23]

Academic discipline was not exacting. Lectures did not begin till half way through the term, and many undergraduates did not come up till then. Those who like Paley lived at a distance would probably stay in residence during vacations,[24] and whether they worked or not would be a matter of their own choice. In the Long Vacation, according to a Christ's undergraduate of a decade before Paley, 'we spend our time, not in a closer application to our books, but in forming schemes for our Diversion and Amusement, which are generally not of the most rational'.[25] The young men were supposed to get up in time for chapel at 7.15 a.m. but they were allowed to miss the service twice a week and Paley always took the opportunity to stay in bed till late in the morning—at the beginning of each week.[26] There were no meals in hall after midday dinner, and tea and supper parties, whether in the host's rooms or in a coffee house, were a regular feature of college life.[27]

Paley was an amusing companion, liked by everyone, the life and soul of any company. His rooms were open to all, though he had the power of abstracting himself from his surroundings, and could sit in a corner reading, oblivious of his friends' company. 'The uncouthness of his dress and manners', we are told, 'caused not a little mirth amongst his fellow collegians, but as the superiority of his genius and his real worth were soon discovered, these singularities did not deprive him of their esteem and admiration.'[28] It would be a mistake to suppose that his rough manners and provincial accent gave him any sense of inferiority or resentment.[29] That sort of social self-consciousness belongs to the nineteenth rather than the eighteenth century, when north-country and other local accents must have been common enough in Cambridge. Perhaps, however, Paley was a little inclined to over-emphasize his rugged provincialism and to parade the low opinion which he held of some of the more polished products of the south. 'A lad came to us at Cambridge,' he said to an old Etonian towards the end of his life; 'he had been seven years at Eton and could not spell *but*.'[30] He liked to speak disrespectfully of lords, and would describe the experience he once had of tutoring a 'foolish nobleman' as worse than dying in a mine from poverty.[31]

There were no examinations until the third year, and consequently there was a strong temptation to postpone serious work until then. Paley was not immune from the temptation. 'I spent the first two years of my undergraduateship', he told a friend in 1795, 'happily but unprofitably. I was constantly in society, where we were not immoral but idle and rather expensive. At the commencement of my third year however, after having left the usual party at rather a late hour in the evening, I was awakened at five in the morning by one of my companions, who stood at my bedside and said: "Paley, I have been thinking what a damned fool you are. I could do nothing, probably, were I to try, and can afford the life I lead; you could do everything and cannot afford it. I have had no sleep during the whole night on account of these reflections and am now come solemnly to inform you that if you persist in your indolence, I must renounce your society." I was so struck with the visit and the visitor that I lay in bed great part of the day and formed my plan. I ordered my bedmaker to prepare my fire every evening, in order that it might be lighted by myself. I arose at five, read during the whole of the day, except such hours as chapel and hall required, allotting to each portion of time its peculiar branch of study; and just before the closing of the gates (nine o'clock) I went to a neighbouring coffee house, where I constantly regaled upon a mutton chop and a dose of milk punch.'[32] Edmund Paley throws doubt on this story, but confirms the general picture of a change to early rising and no social distractions.[33]

In the second term of the third academic year came the exercises known as Acts and Opponencies, oral disputations conducted in Latin. The undergraduate selected as respondent had to submit three theses, usually two mathematical and one philosophical, to be maintained against three opponents. He began by delivering a speech, reading from a prepared text, on any one of the three theses; the first opponent advanced eight arguments in syllogistic form on the other side, the second opponent five and the third three, and the respondent had to answer these arguments as they were advanced.[34] When Paley had to perform his Act, the moderator was Richard Watson. Paley selected a subject from the standard textbook, Johnson's *Quaestiones Philosophicae*, 'Aeternitas poenarum contradicit divinis attributis', and Watson accepted it, as he always accepted any question, whether as moderator or as professor of divinity. Reactions were different in Paley's college. The thesis which the respondent maintained was traditionally the right one, and Paley was proposing to advocate the unorthodox view. A few days afterwards, to quote Watson's own account, 'Paley came to see me in a great fright, saying that the master of his college (Dr Thomas, Dean of Ely) had sent to him and insisted on his not keeping on such a question.'[35] The difficulty was met by the insertion of a *non* into the subject. The future Bishop of Llandaff, who was moderator for Paley's Act, was only a few years older than he, and the two men had some things in common, but they had little personal contact with one another and Paley, who was generally well disposed to his fellow men, maintained a hearty dislike of Watson, a feeling which those who know the latter's autobiography may be disposed to share.[36]

The Acts and Opponencies, though they were still taken seriously and regarded as a valuable exercise, were a survival from the Middle Ages, and their importance was declining in comparison with the written examination in the Senate House, known as the Tripos, which followed a year later. This again was largely mathematical, with, in Paley's day, only an occasional question on philosophy. The examination lasted for two days and a half. It began at 8.00 a.m., and after a break for breakfast from 9.00 a.m. to 9.30 a.m., continued to 11.00 a.m. The afternoon session lasted from 1.30 p.m. to 5.00 p.m. with a half-hour break in the middle, and in the evening there was a two-hour session in the rooms of the Senior Moderator, who regaled the examinees with fruit and wine.[37] The candidates were placed in order of merit, and there was keen competition for the position of Senior Wrangler, or head of the first class. In 1763 the two strongest competitors were Paley and John Frere of Caius, and there was some criticism from Frere's college when Paley appeared at the top of the list, though Frere himself acknowledged that Paley was his superior.[38] This result shows Paley to have been a competent mathematician, but he had no more interest in the subject for its own sake than he had in classics. The intellectual training it gave him may well, however, have left its mark in his lucid, robust, and unimaginative way of thinking.[39]

As Senior Wrangler Paley would naturally expect to have a career in the university; but he was too young for ordination, and had to wait another three years before he got his fellowship. He might perhaps have taken private pupils at Cambridge, though the coach was not then as familiar a feature of the academic world as he later became; but prospects in that field were perhaps too uncertain and he took a post as second assistant at an academy, or private school, at Greenwich, kept by a Mr Bracken. An academy at Greenwich may suggest something like Salem House in *David Copperfield*. But Mr Bracken's establishment, which specialized in preparing boys for the army and navy, probably had greater pretensions than Mr Creakle's; an advertisement of 1782, after Bracken had been succeeded by another headmaster, described it as a long-established academy in which had been educated 'many gentlemen of distinguished rank as well as many celebrated commanders both by land and sea'.[40] It had, however, few attractions for a junior assistant master. 'When I went to town', Paley recalled in later life, 'to teach a school, I pleased my imagination with the delightful task "to teach the young idea how to shoot". The room stank of piss, and a little boy came up as soon as I was seated and began "b, a, b, bab; b, l, e, ble; babble".'[41] He often described his life there as one of 'woful drudgery'; but he was not the sort of man to be discontented with his lot and he is also recorded as having been so happy in his situation that he often said the highest object of his ambition then was to be first instead of second assistant.[42] For recreation he would wander round London, attend the House of Commons or the Law Courts, and go to the theatre. Once when coming out after seeing a play he felt six hands all trying to pick his pockets. They succeeded in taking a handkerchief not worth twopence. 'I was sorry', he said in telling the story, 'for the disappointment of the poor pickpockets.'[43]

Eventually he fell out with the headmaster. He discovered that a lady resident in Greenwich, a widow called Mrs Ord, whose son John was at Bracken's academy, had offered him a position as tutor to her son on condition that he was freed from any engagement to the headmaster, and that Bracken had kept the offer from him.[44] He decided to leave. He had probably given up school-teaching by 23 February 1766, when he was ordained, though a few months short of the canonical age of twenty-three, to the curacy of Greenwich. The ordination took place in Grosvenor Chapel in London and was conducted by the Bishop of Lichfield and Coventry, Frederick Cornwallis, afterwards Archbishop of Canterbury.[45] Greenwich was a valuable Crown living, which would naturally be held by those in favour with the government. The incumbent at the time of Paley's ordination was Samuel Squire, who combined the living with the bishopric of St David's, and John Hinchcliffe, who succeeded Squire on his death in May 1766, was soon to become Master of Trinity and Bishop of Peterborough. These exalted clerics would probably leave much of the work to their curates, and Paley would have been kept fairly busy with parochial duties[46] which, however, did not prevent him from doing what many curates did, supplementing his income by tuition. He set up house on his own, and could not afford the carpet for his stone floor which Mrs Ord thought should be provided for her son; when John Ord first came to his house 'he goodhumouredly and thriftily made him stand on the bellows'.[47] Later in 1766, on 24 June, he was elected fellow of his college. The Master of Christ's and the Tutor, Shepherd, tried to persuade him to come into residence at once, but he considered himself bound by his engagement to Mrs Ord and stayed at Greenwich for another year until his pupil was ready to go up to Christ's as an undergraduate. John Ord was his favourite pupil and remembered him as his 'much loved friend and as it were second father'.[48]

In 1765 Paley had enhanced his reputation in his university by winning the Members' Prize, open to Bachelors, for a Latin essay. The subject set was *Utrum civitati perniciosior sit Epicuri an Zenonis philosophia* (Which is the more harmful to society, the Epicurean or the Stoic philosophy?). Paley wrote his essay in English, then translated it into Latin but left the notes in English; this made one of the examiners suspect that the candidate had been helped by a father who had forgotten his Latin, but the Master of St John's rightly insisted that it would be wrong to reject the essay merely on suspicion and Paley was adjudged the winner.[49] Those who enter for prize essays generally do so more because they want the prize than because they are interested in the subject set, but it can happen that the subject awakes their interest. (This was the case with Thomas Clarkson, whose whole life's work was determined by the fact that when he entered for the Members' Prize the subject set was the slave trade.) Paley's prize essay may well have helped to direct his attention to ethical problems and lead him to the point of view which he afterwards expounded in his published work. It was not his intention, he explained in one of his notes, to defend the principles of either Stoicism or Epicureanism but rather to show the insufficiency of both. 'It was reserved for one greater than Zeno to exalt the dignity of virtue with its utility and by superinducing a future state, to support the paradox of the Stoic on Epicurean principles.'[50] This is more or less the doctrine of his *Moral and Political Philosophy*.

✤2✤
Cambridge

The Cambridge in which Paley took up residence was a predominantly clerical society. Almost all fellows of colleges were obliged to be in orders, and holders of university posts who were not fellows were few and unimportant. The academic clergy were not particularly noted for piety or austerity of life; there were eccentrics and reprobates among them, and men addicted to more or less harmless conviviality. At the same time there were conscientious teachers and men with a real interest in intellectual and religious questions. Until the French Revolution made all such ideas suspect, the tone of the university, or at any rate of its more intellectually alert members, tended to be liberal and reformist.

Fellows of colleges led an easy life, but one which had the disadvantage of obliging them to celibacy. As the Oxford poet Thomas Warton put it:

> But who can bear to waste his whole age
> Amid the dulness of a college,
> Debarr'd the common joys of life,
> And that prime bliss–a loving wife.
> O! What's a table richly spread,
> Without a woman at its head!
> Would some snug benefice but fall,
> Ye feasts, ye dinners! farewell all![1]

The colleges themselves had snug benefices to dispose of, but they were not sufficient to satisfy the demand, and one of the less attractive features of academic life was the constant canvassing of influential patrons by dons anxious for preferment. Gunning records how his father was once with Samuel Ogden of St John's, an uncouth miserly man, when the news came that a certain divine had died. 'Let me see,' said Ogden. 'He had a stall at Canterbury, and two livings, all in the gift of the Crown,—let's try what we can lay our hands upon—take a pen and write as I dictate,' and proceeded to dictate a letter to the Prime Minister beginning 'The great are always liable to importunity; those who are both good and great are liable to a double portion.'[2] Paley, who would have nothing to do with such activities, invented the term 'rooting' for 'that baseness and servility which like swine rooting in a dunghill will perform the basest acts for a rich patron, to gain his protection and a good benefice'.[3] When Pitt visited Cambridge, Paley, who had by then left the university, remarked that if he had been asked to preach before the Prime Minister, he would have chosen as his text: 'There is a lad here who hath five barley loaves and two small fishes, but what are those among so many?'[4]

Thus many of the dons spent much of their time trying to get away. Those who did not succeed in doing so lived a life which, for all its apparent attractions, tended to be unsatisfying. Their love of learning was not always strong enough to sustain them, and the academic world had not yet devised those numerous administrative and tutorial activities which today keep its members busy and happy. The conviviality of the High Table and Combination Room contrasted with the loneliness of the bachelor's rooms.

> When all these forms and duties pass away,
> And the day passes like the former day,
> Then of exterior things at once bereft,
> He's to himself and one attendant left;
> Nay, John too goes; nor aught of service more
> Remains for him; he gladly quits the door,
> And as he whistles to the college-gate,
> He kindly pities his poor master's fate.[5]

And there were some fellows of colleges whose fate was more pitiable than that of the lonely bachelor with not enough to occupy him. In 1768, when the Master and six senior fellows of St John's met to appoint to two vacancies in their number, they agreed 'that the insanity of the two fellows next to the seniority, Mr Allen and Mr Stubbs, is a weighty cause why they should not be elected into the number of seniors'.[6]

Many fellows, however, left their colleges for marriage and a benefice. To Adam Smith this was a matter of regret, since the Church drew off from the university its ablest members.[7] On the other hand it was not wholly disadvantageous to the university; it meant that there was plenty of scope for young men in college teaching and administration, and young men may well be better teachers of the young than the elderly, however distinguished. After coming into residence Paley was appointed to various posts in Christ's. In 1767 he became Praelector, Junior Dean, and Catechist, and Bunting, Walhampton, and Knapwell preacher, to which offices were added in the next year those of Steward and Hebrew lecturer. From 1768 to 1770 he was Senior Greek Lecturer and Mildmay preacher; in 1771 he was appointed Custos Cistae and in 1775 Senior Dean. He held the office of Taxor for the year 1770–1, a university post to which the colleges nominated in turn and which involved inspection of weights and measures in the town.[8] Some of his college posts were probably sinecures, for instance, the lectureship in Hebrew, a language of which he is said to have been ignorant.[9] What was important was his tutorial work. In August 1768, when Backhouse, who had been one of the tutors in Paley's undergraduate days, left Cambridge and vacated his office, the other tutor, Shepherd, employed Paley and his friend John Law as his assistants, and in March 1772 they became joint tutors.

Paley's friendship with Law determined the course of his later life. They had overlapped for a year as undergraduates at Christ's and had been slightly acquainted then; after Law's election to a fellowship in 1770 they became close friends and they remained so throughout life. They collaborated as tutors in term time and they explored the country together in vacations. Law was described by Boswell as 'a man of great variety of knowledge, uncommon genius and, I believe, sincere religion'.[10] He did not achieve the fame of his brother Edward, the first Lord Ellenborough (also a friend of Paley's); he wrote no books and he rose no higher in the Church than the Irish bishopric of Elphin. But, according to one writer, though he was younger than Paley, there was something in him which 'without either effort or intention, in the early days of their friendship acquired and long maintained a high ascendant over the mind of Paley'.[11]

Through John Law Paley got to know his father Edmund, Master of Peterhouse and from 1769 Bishop of Carlisle, a post which he combined with his Mastership. Edmund Law, like Paley, was the son of a north-country clergyman and schoolmaster. He wrote a number of theological works, some of which are not entirely forgotten.[12] He was by temperament a retiring scholar, latitudinarian in his views, a believer in freedom of inquiry, and always tolerant of others' opinions. To quote from the brief memoir which Paley wrote of him, 'He was zealously attached to religious liberty, because he thought that it leads to truth; yet from his heart he loved peace. . . . He was a man of great softness of manners and of the mildest and most tranquil disposition. His voice was never raised above its ordinary pitch. His countenance seemed never to have been ruffled; it preserved the same kind and composed aspect, truly indicating the calmness and benignity of his temper.'[13] His researches, Paley wrote elsewhere, had 'never lost sight of one purpose, namely, to recover the simplicity of the gospel from beneath that load of unauthorized additions, which the ignorance of some ages, and the learning of others, the superstition of weak and the craft of designing men have (unhappily for its interest) heaped upon it'.[14] Though he did not endorse all Bishop Law's views, Paley was a good deal influenced by him, and it was to him that he owed his early preferments in the Church.

As Tutor of Christ's Paley interviewed and examined candidates for admission, saw them individually when they came into residence, invited them to breakfast, and took them out for walks. He advised them on their studies and on their general conduct, recommending them, for instance, not to refuse the loan of a few pounds to a fellow-student, 'because if the young man be good for anything, he will repay you; and if he is not, he will no longer frequent your society; and you will get cheaply rid of a worthless companion'.[15] In fact he was a tutor in the best traditions of the office—or perhaps we should say that he anticipated what later became a tradition. If it were not for the absence of vacation reading parties, we might almost be in Jowett's Balliol.

The tutors' teaching duties were divided between Paley and John Law, Law taking mathematics and natural philosophy and Paley metaphysics, ethics, and the Greek Testament. For ethics, on which he lectured to the second and third years, he used no textbook, but compiled his own material, which he later wrote up in his book *Moral and Political Philosophy*. For metaphysics his text for first-year students was Locke's *Essay concerning Human Understanding*, after which he went on to Samuel Clarke's *On the Being and Attributes of God*. His Greek Testament lectures, which took place on Sundays and

Wednesdays at 8.0 p.m., were attended by all undergraduates. In addition he gave, in 1775 and 1776, a course of Divinity lectures for B.A.s who were intending to be ordained, a useful innovation at a time when a large proportion of the students were destined for Holy Orders and no professional training was provided by the Church.[16]

Among Paley's pupils was William Frend, who later became notorious for his religious and political unorthodoxy and was tried before the Vice-Chancellor and expelled from the university in 1793. In a letter to his daughter written many years later Frend recalls the impression made on him by Paley when he went up to Christ's. 'The first time I saw him was on my admission at College, when I deliver'd to him a letter of introduction from the then archdeacon of Canterbury, and in a very little time got over the little agitation which a young man naturally feels at an examination. My father of course was not present, but Paley dined with us at the Master's Lodge, where was a mixed party, and he would have taken us to his room for supper if my father had not collected a set of younkers with whom to spend the evening. My next interview with him was on coming to reside, when I drank tea with him and sat upwards of two hours with him tête à tête, during which he settled everything for my lodgement that night in College, and the next day he put me under the care of a proper young man to introduce me into the hall, and after this I was a constant attendant on his lectures, which were scarcely ever shirked by any one as they were a treat in themselves.'[17]

Frend was probably the author of an excellent account of Paley's teaching—a more appropriate word in his case than lecturing—published by an old pupil who signed himself 'A Christian'.[18] Paley, he says, was not content to read out from his notes; he did his best to arouse interest by questioning his class. He kept them amused, but knew when to be serious. There was no need for compulsion or punishment to ensure attendance; it was sufficient punishment to be unable to attend.[19] 'You should have seen him ... when he stepped out of his little study into the lecture room, rolled from the door into his arm chair, turned his old scratch over his left ear' [a scratch is a small wig; the lecture room would be the large room, part of Paley's set, into which his study opened] 'and put his left leg over his right, buttoned up his waistcoat, pulled up a stocking, and fixed a dirty, cover-torn, ragged Locke upon his left knee, moistened his thumb with his lip, and then turned over the ragged leaves of his books, dogseared and scrawled about, with the utmost rapidity.'[20] After settling himself down he began to ask questions on the previous lecture. 'Pray Mr B—(to a freshman) give me an instance of a simple idea.' B. answers, "The Vice-Chancellor." 'Very well, very well, Mr B.— and now tell me what you mean by the Vice-Chancellor.' After a pause Paley goes on to ask if Mr B. has seen the Vice-Chancellor, and when he reluctantly answers "Yes," 'poor fellow, it was now all over with him: the beadles, the silver maces, the large cap, large band, great wig, solemn port and a few goodly allusions to the dignified person of the Vice-Chancellor, all come forth, and not one person who hears that lecture will mistake a complex for a simple idea'. After the questions on the previous lecture, 'Paley's position in his seat was changed; the scratch, the leg, the book, took exactly the opposite directions, the thumb was moistened as before, the leaves turned over, but nine times out of ten not stopped at the place which had any reference to what he was going to say, when in the most familiar manner he discussed some subject in moral philosophy, pointing out the passages we were to read for the next lecture day and explaining everything in such a manner that the driest subjects were made interesting'.

In the Greek Testament class each student was put on in turn to translate, but there was also comment from the lecturer. 'We had not, you may be sure, any rigmarole stories about the Trinity, or such stuff; the five points' [the points in dispute between Calvinists and Arminians] 'were left to repose in antiquated folios; the Thirty-nine Articles were never hinted at; the creed of Calvin . . . was never thought of; and Paley seems to have taken throughout for his model Locke on the Reasonableness of Christianity and his comments on the Epistles.' The great point on which he insisted was 'that we should listen to God, not to man; that we should exert our faculties in under-standing the language of holy men of old; that we should free ourselves, as much as possible, from all prejudices of birth, education and country; and we should not call any our master in religion but Jesus Christ'.

Paley's son questions this account on the ground that the Greek Testament from which his father lectured was chiefly filled with critical and explanatory notes.[21] But though the account may be coloured by the writer's own views, it is in line with the advice given in a document dating from Paley's Cambridge days, which Edmund Paley himself reproduces, in which after giving directions on the study of the New Testament Paley writes:

> In examining any point of controversy (which by the by may be deferred till you have completed or made a considerable progress in the above prescribed course) I would advise you, before you take up a book on either side of the question, to read the New Testament from beginning to end with a view solely to that one subject; and collect all the texts as you go along, which appear to have any the most distant relation to it. Afterwards reduce the number of these texts by striking out such as are found, upon a second examination, to have no *real* connexion with the subject, and then carefully peruse the remainder with the notes, comments and assistances I suppose you now possessed of. Thus you will be enabled either to form a judgment of the question from what you have before you, or at least to read the books that are written upon it with edification and pleasure.[22]

In the same way Locke, whose influence was as strong on Paley as on eighteenth-century thought in general, decided in view of 'the little satisfaction and consistency that is to be found in most of the systems of divinity' to betake himself 'to the sole reading of Scripture (to which they all appeal) for the understanding the Christian religion'.[23]

Paley's period of residence at Cambridge coincided with a movement for reform within and without the university. Two questions were taken up by the reformers, one partly, the other wholly concerned with the university. The first was the question of subscription to the Thirty-nine Articles, the second the reform of university studies and the examination system. On both points the leader of the reforming party was John Jebb, of whom it was said that as soon as he got to heaven he would find something there in need of reform. Jebb[24] was an under-graduate at Peterhouse, Edmund Law's college, was elected fellow in 1760, and was ordained two years later. In 1764 he vacated his fellow-ship by marriage, but after a year away from Cambridge returned to the university and taught as a private tutor. His wife shared his views and supported his schemes for reform with her pen. This childless couple, liberal, progressive, conscientious, seem to belong to the Cambridge of the later nineteenth rather than the eighteenth century, though if Jebb had lived a century later, he would probably have moved even further away from orthodox Christianity than he did.

The movement for relief from subscription had two aspects, of which one concerned the Church as a whole and the other the university. The reformers wanted the clergy to be free from the obligation to assent to the Articles; they also wished to put an end to subscription in the universities. At Cambridge, the university which concerns us and the one where the reformers were vocal and influential, the obligation dated from the time of James I, who had required all candidates for degrees to subscribe to the Royal Supremacy, the Book of Common Prayer, and the Thirty-nine Articles.[25] The last of these requirements was the particular concern of the reformers.

There was already some opposition to subscription when in 1757 Dr Powell of St John's, later to be one of the strongest opponents of the reforming group, preached a sermon justifying subscription but allowing some latitude in its interpretation.[26] He was answered by Francis Blackburne, rector of Richmond, Yorks, and archdeacon of Cleveland, who then proceeded, with the encouragement of Edmund Law, to write a book, *The Confessional*, setting out his views in full and arguing that the clergy should only be required to affirm their belief in the Scriptures. It was Blackburne who, early in 1771, drew up proposals for a petition for relief to be presented to Parliament. Meetings were held in London at the Feathers Tavern to draft the petition and to organize support for it. Jebb, it need hardly be said, was one of Blackburne's active supporters. Edmund Law was sympathetic, but remained in the background. It was said that he had not enough resolution to declare himself openly; but his son, John, attended one of the meetings and this was taken to indicate the Bishop's support.[27]

Though they were active in canvassing, the petitioners obtained the support of only about two hundred and fifty signatories, including some lawyers and physicians who, not without reason, opposed the imposition of subscription on candidates for degrees in their faculties. In their petition they claimed the right of each man to judge for himself what might be proved from scripture. The Articles, they maintained, were drawn up by fallible men, and to subscribe to them discouraged free inquiry and caused division and mutual dislike between Protestants. They begged for relief from 'an obligation so incongruous with the right of private judgment, so pregnant with danger to true religion, and so productive of distress to many pious and conscientious men and useful subjects of the state'.[28] The petition was presented to Parliament in February 1772; it was debated and rejected by 217 votes to 71.

Meanwhile the domestic issue had been taken up at Cambridge in advance of parliamentary action. In December 1771 a proposal to relieve B.A.s from subscription was unanimously rejected by the Caput, a kind of steering committee for the Senate, on the ground that 'the university had no power of making so material a change; and that the times were not favourable to so great an undertaking, which required the slow and wise deliberations of the supreme legislature, not the partial determination of a few academics'.[29] A little later a petition got up by an objectionable Fellow Commoner of Queens', Charles Crawford,[30] and signed by a number of undergraduates, was presented to the Vice-Chancellor. The petitioners claimed that the undergraduates had so much work to do that there was no time to inquire into abstruse theological questions. They asked for relief from subscription, or if this could not be effected, that 'such timely assistance may be afforded in their respective colleges as will enable your petitioners to satisfy their consciences in subscribing them'.[31] In an interview with the Vice-Chancellor Crawford claimed that the petitioners did not object to any of the Articles but only to signing them when they had had no opportunity to study them.[32] The ingenuous attitude of Crawford and the skilful phrasing of the petition were probably inspired by Jebb, who published a series of letters on the subject in which, while not hiding his own dislike of the articles, he urged the students of Cambridge to study them and seek instruction on them.[33] There must have been many dons who, if not themselves opposed to subscription, did not relish the idea of having to expound the Articles to their students.

At first the university authorities thought they had no power to alter a requirement imposed as a result of a Royal Command. The lawyers, however, reassured them on this point, and in March 1772 a syndicate (the Cambridge term for a committee) was appointed to consider the matter. Things now moved quickly. On 23 June it was resolved in the case of B.A.s to substitute for subscription to the Articles the formula 'I declare that I am, *bona fide*, a member of the Church of England as by law established'. The cynical might call this a clever out-manoeuvring of the undergraduate petitioners. In fact it was a reasonable compromise. Cambridge was not yet ready for the idea of a non-Anglican, much less a secular, university. It was only in 1871, almost a hundred years after the petition was presented, that religious tests were finally abolished at Cambridge. Ninety-nine years is a short time in the life of a university. It is even shorter in the life of the Church, which has had to wait for more than twice as long for the abolition of clerical subscription to the Articles, and is still waiting.[34]

Where did Paley stand in all this? There is no doubt that he was on the side of the reformers. When, however, he was invited to sign the petition, he declined, remarking that he could not afford to keep a conscience.[35] This remark did Paley harm in some quarters. 'I never thought Paley an honest man,' said Dr Parr. 'He could not afford forsooth to keep a conscience; and he had none.'[36] Parr's condemnation came ill from one who, as he himself put on record, had 'refused to act with Dr Jebb'.[37] Paley's son considered that too much had been made of a remark which was not meant seriously.[38] Another defendant of Paley, justly observing that he was a man 'of the most unvarnished honesty', thought that his refusal must have been due to disapproval of the petition itself or of the methods or personalities of those who organized it.[39] It is certainly true that remarks of Paley made in jest were sometimes taken too seriously; such remarks, as one writer puts it, 'though at the time sufficiently secured ... from misapprehension by the nod, or wink, or wreathed smile, that accompanied them, were liable to be clothed by malice with an unintended meaning: or might, by a grave and slower mind, like that of Parr, be actually misunderstood'.[40] It is also true that others who were in general sympathy with the petitioners declined to join them, Parr because they 'grasped too much at once', and Watson because he did not wholly approve their manner of proceeding.[41] But if Paley had such reservations he did not reveal them.

The petition gave rise to a number of sermons, charges, and pamphlets on both sides. Edmund Law remained on the side of reform, and in 1774 published 'Considerations on the Propriety of requiring Subscription to Articles of Faith'. He was answered by Thomas Randolph, President of Corpus Christi, Oxford, in a charge 'The Reasonableness of Subscription to Articles of Religion', which provoked an immediate reply from Paley in his 'Defence of the Considerations on the Propriety of requiring a Subscription to Articles of Faith, in Reply to a late Answer from the Clarendon Press'. This was published anonymously as the work of 'a Friend of Religious Liberty'. According to one writer it shows strong internal evidence of Paley's authorship; according to another internal evidence is strongly against the ascription.[42] Fortunately there is no need to rely on internal evidence; Paley's son who was, if anything, disposed to play down his father's unorthodoxy, states categorically that the pamphlet was his work.[43] It is a work of controversy, a reply to a reply, answering in turn his opponent's arguments. It shows clearly enough that he supported the principles behind the petition to Parliament, though not necessarily the abolition of all tests.

> Let the Church [he writes] discharge from her liturgy controversies unconnected with devotion; let her try what may be done for all sides, by worshipping God in that generality of expression in which he himself has left some points; let her dismiss many of her Articles, and convert those which she retains into terms of peace; let her recall the terrors she suspended over freedom of inquiry; let the toleration she extends to dissenters be made 'absolute'; let her invite men to search the Scriptures; let her governors encourage the studious and learned of all persuasions:—Let her do this—and she will be secure of the thanks of her own clergy, and, what is more, of their sincerity. A greater consent may grow out of inquiry than many at present are aware of; and the few who, after all, shall think it necessary to recede from our communion, will acknowledge the necessity to be inevitable; will respect the equity and moderation of the established Church, and live in peace with all its members.[44]

In his *Moral and Political Philosophy*, published in 1785, Paley included a brief chapter on subscription.[45] He argued that the essential point was the intention of the imposer of subscription, the legislature of 1571.

> Those who contend, that nothing less can justify subscription to the Thirty-nine Articles, than the actual belief of each and every separate proposition contained in them, must suppose, that the legislature expected the consent of ten thousand men, and that in perpetual succession [i.e., the clergy of the day and their successors]

not to one controverted proposition, but to many hundreds. It is difficult to conceive how this could be expected by any, who observed the incurable diversity of human opinion upon all subjects short of demonstration.

The intention of the legislature, in Paley's view, was to exclude from offices in the Church all abettors of popery, Anabaptists, and Puritans, and others hostile to the English Church as established; it was legitimate for all except those who fell within these categories to subscribe. And when approached by an inquirer in 1788 he replied that, after much consideration, he maintained the view he had expressed in his book three years earlier. He admitted that the terms of subscription seemed to require a positive assent to every proposition in the Articles, but held that 'private persons acting under the direction of a law may be said to do their duty if they act up to what they believe to be the design of the legislature in making the law; whether their opinion of that design be founded upon the terms of the statute alone or upon the nature of the subject and the actual probability'.[46]

Paley's chapter on subscription aroused a good deal of criticism. His biographer Meadley calls it 'the gangrene of his work'.[47] The embittered radical Gilbert Wakefield wrote in his usual intemperate way: 'I blush for this degradation of my species ... when I see that author stain the pages of his incomparable book with such a shuffling chapter'.[48] Another writer more reasonably described it as 'the last effort of an ingenious mind to soften the rigours of a practice which he could not seriously approve, but which he could not effectively alter', and 'a guide to people, not how they may believe before they subscribe, but how they may subscribe without a very hearty assent'.[49] It should be read in conjunction with Paley's treatment of the same subject from a different point of view elsewhere in the same book.[50] Here he allows that the existence of an established religion made it essential to impose some test on its ministers. Though such tests might be of some use in promoting order and tranquillity, they had serious disadvantages. 'They check inquiry; they violate liberty; they ensnare the conscience of the clergy by holding out temptations to prevarication.' It might not follow that they ought to be abolished; but they should be made as simple and easy as possible, and should be revised as circumstances change. A promise of conformity to the liturgy of the Church, or 'articles of peace'—promises, that is, not to preach certain doctrines or revive certain controversies—might serve the purpose of the existing tests. 'In a word, it ought to be held a sufficient reason for relaxing the terms of subscription or for dropping all or any of the articles to be subscribed, that no *present* necessity requires the strictness which is complained of, or that it should be extended to so many points of doctrine.'

The other question taken up by the reformers in the 1770s, the Cambridge examination system, had already been raised before Paley's return to Cambridge, when Watson, in a speech of 1766, advocated annual examinations for all students, including noblemen and fellow commoners.[51] In 1772 Jebb started a campaign for reform.[52] In November of that year he approached the Vice-Chancellor, who was sympathetic, but took no action. Then in April 1773 Jebb published his 'Remarks upon the Present Mode of Education in the University of Cambridge, to which is added a Proposal for its Improvement'. He had no wish to alter the existing degree examinations. His objection to the system was that it encouraged idleness in the early part of an undergraduate career, followed in the last year by 'an obstinate course of labours which enfeeble the mental powers of the student, at the same time that they have not unfrequently been known to be destructive of his health'.[53] He also criticized the narrowness of the curriculum, which led to the virtual neglect of subjects other than mathematics. His proposal was that there should be annual examinations for all undergraduates, to include the law of nature and of nations, chronology, history (with prescribed periods), classics (with prescribed books), mathematics, metaphysics, natural and moral philosophy. He won a good deal of support in the university and also inevitably aroused opposition. In the course of the year a number of Graces (the Cambridge term for proposals to the Senate) were put forward and rejected. Finally in February 1774 Jebb was successful to the extent that the Senate approved a Grace proposing the appointment of a syndicate to consider the question. The syndicate, of which Paley was a member, reported in March. It made two main proposals. The first was that noblemen and fellow commoners should be examined each year by the university, in the first year on classics, ancient history, composition, and algebra; in the second on the same subjects with the addition of Locke's *Essay on the Human Understanding* and natural philosophy;

and in the third on natural philosophy, natural law, and modern history. The other proposal was that the rest of the undergraduates should (in addition to the existing examinations) be examined in their second year on classics, ancient history, composition, geometry, algebra, and logic. These proposals, though they had substantial support, were rejected by a majority in the Senate.

Jebb was not discouraged, and soon came forward with new proposals. Those of the syndicate were open to criticism in that they prescribed special examinations for noblemen and fellow commoners. The argument that 'the views and pursuits of the students of the higher orders being naturally different from those of inferior degree, it was reasonable that their course of study should also be different', and that 'students of family and fortune would be discouraged by the too possible ill-success of their labours',[54] hardly justified the perpetuation of an academic anomaly. Even Jebb, however, did not propose the complete abolition of class distinction. His new plan, published in August 1774, proposed a single first examination for all students, but a special second one for noblemen and fellow commoners. This proposal was lost by only one vote. Jebb continued his efforts, but he had for some time been moving in the direction of Unitarianism, and in 1775 he resigned his church appointments and the next year he moved to London. His defection from the Church lost him all influence in the university.

There were some who opposed the reformers simply from dislike of any change, or from dislike of Jebb.[55] Others disapproved of examinations because they encouraged a spirit of emulation, though this argument could well have been used against the highly competitive Tripos examination already in existence. The strongest opposition, however, came from supporters of college teaching, who disliked a plan which would have weakened the position of college tutors. Conservatism and a belief in the college system combined in Jebb's strongest opponent, Dr Powell, Master of St John's, an orthodox and autocratic churchman and Tory, who had introduced into his own college in 1766 a scheme by which undergraduates were examined twice yearly and which might be held to make the proposed university examinations unnecessary. The example of St John's was followed at Trinity towards the end of the century when annual college examinations were introduced, and in the early part of the nineteenth century some of the smaller colleges followed suit. But eventually the university moved in the direction indicated by the reformers of the 1770s. In 1822 it was decided to introduce a 'Previous Examination' in the fifth term of residence, and three years later noblemen lost their old privilege of taking their degrees without examination.[56]

Paley was a supporter of Jebb's schemes. As we have seen, he was on the syndicate appointed to consider examination reform, and he was one of those who voted in favour of Jebb's revised plan.[57] He thought that the existing system put too much strain on undergraduates. 'You may do anything,' he said, 'with young men by encouragement, by prizes, honours, and distinctions. See what is done at Cambridge. But there the stimulus is too strong; two or three heads are cracked by it every year.... Why, some of them go mad; others are reduced to such a state of debility, both of mind and body, that they are unfit for anything during the rest of their lives.'[58] He was in favour of broadening the curriculum and making all undergraduates subject to examination. But, he said, 'one thing I always set my face against; and that is exercises in English composition: this calling upon lads ... for a style before they have got ideas, sets them upon fine writing, and is the main cause of the puffy, spungy, spewy, washy style that prevails at the present day'.[59] If the 'composition' included in the syndicate's proposals meant English and not Latin composition, he was evidently unable to bring his fellow-syndics over to his view.

In all ages men have liked to label their fellow countrymen as belonging to this or that party, Whig or Tory, reformer or conservative, progressive or reactionary. Paley was not, and is not, easily labelled. When the Jebbs first met him, they did not quite know what to make of him, but had hopes that he would turn out liberal in his views.[60] George Dyer, with some hesitation, classed him among the 'Cambridge Reformers'.[61] On the other hand Edmund Law expressed the fear that his influence on his son, Lord Ellenborough, would counteract his own and make him a Tory rather than a Whig.[62] Paley in fact was not a party man. He went his own way, and though certainly liberal-minded, was no doctrinaire reformer and in politics was generally speaking content with things as they were. In later life he used to recall with pleasure his conversations with Jebb and others. They had no idea, he said, that they were talking treason—treason, that is, by the standards of the period of reaction that followed the French Revolution. He himself, he said, had always been an advocate of 'bribery and corruption', and when his companions protested had said: 'Why, who is so mad as to expect to be governed by force? Or who is such a fool as to expect to be governed by virtue? There remains nothing but bribery and corruption'.[63]

These discussions took place at the Hyson Club, which had been founded in 1758[64] and whose members met to drink hyson (a kind of china tea) and to talk. No particular subjects were proposed for discussion; 'the conversation was that of literary men unbending themselves'.[65] Among the members was Edward Waring of Magdalene, a distinguished mathematician and a close friend of Paley's.[66] Jebb and other reformers belonged, but there were also men of a different way of thinking, such as John Gordon of Peterhouse, a Tory who was regularly worsted in his arguments with Jebb, and Isaac Milner of Queens', who was the only undergraduate of his college who refused to sign the petition for relief from subscription.[67]

In his own college Paley was, as he had been in undergraduate days, a popular member of the society. Though he was often late for dinner in hall, 'some repartee amply repaid the upper table for the delay, and its festivity was communicated to every region of the hall'.[68] His geniality and good humour did not, however, stop him from standing up for his principles when he thought it necessary. Shepherd, the tutor whom he and Law assisted and later succeeded, was a man who made up for some deficiencies in scholarship by his knowledge of the world, his business acumen, and his musical ability, which commended him to the powerful Earl of Sandwich.[69] In 1771 a concert was arranged in the hall of Christ's under the patronage of Sandwich. Paley and Law insisted that the concert be cancelled unless an undertaking was given that Sandwich's mistress, the singer Martha Ray, should not attend, and Shepherd reluctantly agreed.[70] Another incident of college life shows how Paley combined justice with mercy. One of the college servants was found to have committed thefts; Paley instituted proceedings against him, but at the same time paid for counsel to defend him. He explained that he considered it his duty to society and to the college to institute proceedings; 'but let the fellow have fair play in his trial and if through any of the loopholes of the law he then escape conviction, I have done my duty and shall be content'. The servant did escape conviction.[71] Yet another story from his Cambridge days illustrates his remarkable good nature. He used to fish in the Cam, which must have provided poor sport by comparison with the streams of his home country in the north. On one occasion when he was fishing, a butcher's boy appeared on horseback on the other side of the river, wanting to cross but afraid to do so. Paley told him where he could get across higher up, and the boy offered him a penny if he would carry his tray over the river while he jumped over on his horse. Paley took the tray, even though it meant wading across with the water nearly up to his breast.[72]

Paley was eminently successful in his work at Christ's. While he and Law were tutors the reputation of the college stood high. 'Every chamber,' we read, 'was filled, and their pupils overflowed into lodgings in the town. Many of these pupils were men of great fortune who besides paying largely to the public tutor, paid in addition for private instructions.'[73] In actual fact, as the Register of Admissions shows, there was no dramatic rise in numbers during Paley's tutorship, but the statement quoted, even if exaggerated, at least shows what people thought and said at the time.[74]

Rewarding though his life at Cambridge was, Paley had never intended to stay there. In talking to his friends he would dwell on the pleasures of a country clergyman's life, and he made no secret of his intention of leaving the university as soon as he could.[75] He had been ordained priest on 21 December 1767, by the Bishop of London, on Letters Dimissory from the Bishop of Ely,[76] and while at Cambridge he had some experience of the ecclesiastical world of London as one of the 'Whitehall Preachers'. After the destruction by fire of the old Chapel Royal in Whitehall the Banqueting House was fitted up as a chapel, and in 1724 George I established a system by which twenty-four clerics, twelve from each university, officiated in the chapel, each for half a month; they were appointed by the Bishop of London as Dean of the Chapel Royal from the resident fellows at a salary of £30 per annum.[77] Paley had been a Whitehall Preacher from 1771 and would thus be known in London. But he was not destined to be one of the metropolitan clergy; his association with Bishop Law took him back to the north. He had already served as Law's chaplain on his annual visits to Carlisle, when in May 1775 he was presented by the Bishop to a living in that diocese. He kept his fellowship for another year and finally left Cambridge in the summer of 1776.

He retained pleasant memories of Cambridge and of his friends in the university. But he was aware of the dangers of academic life and the low standards of conduct of some of the dons. In 1795 he preached a sermon before the university in which he spoke of the 'moral debility that arises from the want of being trained in the virtues of active life' and observed that this was something to which men of learning were particularly prone. He also reminded his hearers of 'our Lord's solemn declaration that contumacious knowledge and neglected talents, knowledge which does not lead to obedience, and talents which rest in useless speculations, will be found, in the day of final account, amongst the objects of his severest displeasure'. And he added some weighty words on the harm done to learning by the moral failings of those who professed it.

> Irregular morals in men of distinguished attainments, render them, not despised (for talents and learning can never be despicable) but subjects of malicious remark, perhaps of affected pity, to the enemies of intellectual liberty, of science and literature; and at the same time of sincere, though silent regret, to those who are desirous of supporting the esteem which ought to await the successful pursuit of ingenious studies. We entreat such men to reflect, that their conduct will be made the reply of idleness to industry, the revenge of dulness and ignorance upon parts and learning; to consider, how many will seek, and think they find, in their example, an apology for sloth, and for indifference to all liberal improvement; what a theme, lastly, they supply to those, who, in the discouragement of every mental exertion, preach up the vanity of human knowledge, and the danger or the mischief of superior attainments.[78]

The Diocese of Carlisle

Paley's first benefice was the rectory of Great Musgrave, a village in Westmorland between Kirkby Stephen and Appleby, with a church pleasantly situated on the bank of the river Eden. John Law reported on the value of the living and its attractive situation, and Paley's father on a visit to Cambridge confirmed his favourable report. 'The late rector', wrote Paley to Law, 'saved £3000 out of it in 19 years, besides keeping the best tap of ale in the country. My father never drank any so good.'[1] In May 1775 Paley was there for his induction and found it 'a very pretty place and some of the views from the hill equal to anything I ever saw', with fishing, if poaching could be stopped, the best in England.[2] A year later he moved from Cambridge to take charge of his parish.

Probably he had always regarded marriage as the natural concomitant of a country parson's life, but he had no one in mind as his future wife when he accepted Musgrave. While at Carlisle, however, in connection with his induction he met Jane Hewitt, the daughter of a spirit merchant of the city, and was much struck by her good looks. After a brief consultation with John Law and later on one not much longer with the lady he decided to marry her.[3] His 'very businesslike' love letters were preserved in the family in a little embroidered case.[4] The marriage took place on 6 June 1776, in St Mary's, Carlisle, the parish church which was then housed in the truncated nave of the cathedral.

In spite of the charms of Great Musgrave and in spite of his professed ambition to live the life of a country clergyman Paley was not, it seems, prepared to bury himself in a remote village. He took up his residence in the neighbouring town of Appleby and served his parish from there with the aid of a curate[5] until the next year, when he was presented by the Dean and Chapter of Carlisle, of which John Law was now an influential member, to the living of St Laurence in Appleby itself and resigned from Great Musgrave.[6] Appleby is a pleasant market town, and there Paley spent, so he used to say, some of the happiest years of his life. Apart from the pleasures of marriage and parenthood he could enjoy fishing in the Eden and satisfy his social instincts in a club which met for whist and talk.[7] He found too a congenial companion in an aged and worthy schoolmaster, Richard Yates, master of the grammar school, whose memorial, with an inscription composed by Paley, can be seen in St Laurence's church.

In 1776 Paley was presented by the Bishop to another living, the vicarage of Dalston, a fair-sized village four miles south of Carlisle, on the river Caldew, with a church which had been largely rebuilt some twenty-five years before Paley's incumbency. He did not, however, take up residence there until 1780, and soon after doing so he was appointed to the fourth prebendal stall in Carlisle cathedral. He retained the living of Appleby until 1785, but apparently did not reside there after 1780. Both his biographers were incorrectly informed on this point. Meadley states that his connection with Appleby terminated in 1782, when he became archdeacon, Edmund Paley that after holding the living for about three years, he gave it up to enable the Bishop to provide for a relation;[8] the episcopal registers establish the date of his resignation as 1785. From 1780 he had two houses, his prebendal residence in the cathedral close, which he enlarged to accommodate his growing family, and the vicarage at Dalston, where he had twenty acres of glebe which he farmed without success.

In Dalston parish was Rose Castle, the episcopal palace, and Paley was thus able to keep in close touch with Bishop Law and his son John, who had now become archdeacon. In 1782 John Law was appointed to the Irish bishopric of Clonfert. Paley preached at his consecration in Dublin Castle chapel, and accompanied him to County Galway for his enthronement, at which there was the unprecedently large congregation of sixteen.[9] Law moved to Killala in 1787 and to Elphin in 1795. He was in his diocese when the Irish rebellion of 1798 broke out. 'The Popish multitude', writes the nineteenth-century historian of the Church of Ireland, ' ... were on the point of joining the insurgents. ... But the evil was counteracted by the magnanimity and fortitude of the bishop, Dr Law; who fortified his palace, resolutely maintained his post, bade defiance to the rebels, animated the loyal gentry and the well-disposed inhabitants by his example, and by his wise and seasonable exertions was the means, under Divine Providence, of preserving the property and lives of the protestants of that county [Roscommon] from the outrages of a deluded and infuriated multitude.'[10] Law shared the liberal principles of his father and put them into practice. He supported in the Irish House of Lords the Bill of 1793 which gave the franchise to Roman Catholics.[11] At Killala he decided that as it was a hopeless task to make his people Protestants he would do his best to make them good Catholics, and had printed at his own expense and distributed free in his diocese the works of a Catholic writer 'which breathe the piety, and in plain and intelligible language inculcate the morality of the Bible'.[12] His liberality extended to Joseph Priestley, whose religious and political views most churchmen regarded as highly dangerous; when Priestley was forced to leave England for America Law sent him an anonymous gift of £100.[13]

On his promotion to a bishopric Law vacated his archdeaconry and Paley succeeded him. Before its enlargement at the expense of Chester in 1856, Carlisle was a small and compact diocese with only one arch-deacon. His position, however, was peculiar. He had the right of examining and presenting candidates for ordination and of inducting those instituted to benefices, but the other archidiaconal functions had passed into the hands of the chancellor of the diocese.[14] In 1785, however, Paley succeeded to the chancellorship, retaining his arch-deaconry. The chancellor conducted visitations, and in the years when the bishop did not hold a visitation these occasions were used for the delivery of charges.[15] Paley's charges were partly concerned with practical matters, the duties of churchwardens, the remuneration of parish clerks, the desirability of inserting in baptismal registers the mother's maiden name. But he also spoke on the studies appropriate to the clergy and their ministerial duties; on one occasion, when he took as his subject 'The Use and Propriety of Local and Occasional Preaching', he explained that as he was archdeacon as well as chan-cellor he felt at liberty to address the clergy as an archdeacon would have done in any other diocese.[16]

To the archdeaconry was annexed the living of Great Salkeld, a village on the Eden about halfway between Appleby and Carlisle. Opposite to Great Salkeld, on the other side of the river, is the parish of Addingham,[17] which he added to his preferments in 1792. Evidently he did not reside in either of these parishes. In 1793 he was appointed

to Stanwix, a village, as it then was, across the river from Carlisle, with
a church on the site of a Roman fort and built with its materials, but in
Paley's day 'gloomy, being only part of the original structure'.[18] He
now gave up the vicarage of Dalston. There were, he explained, three
reasons for making the change. The first was that it saved double
housekeeping, since Stanwix was within twenty minutes' walk from
his prebendal house; the second was that the living was fifty pounds
more in value; thirdly, 'I began to find my stock of sermons coming
over again too fast'.[19]

As Paley himself, though by no means mean or avaricious, was not
indifferent to money, it is appropriate to follow the example of his first
biographer and record the value of the various posts he held. Musgrave
was worth £80, Appleby £200 and Dalston £90. His prebend brought
him £400 and the archdeaconry (i.e., the living of Great Salkeld) £120.
The income of the chancellorship was variable, but not less than £100,
and Addingham and Stanwix were each worth £140. According to his
son, it was only in the latter part of his residence in Cumberland that
he had as much as £500 from his preferments.[20] But he must have
reached this figure in 1780, when he was made a prebendary, and at the
end of his period in the diocese, when he held the prebend, the archdeaconry, the chancellorship, and the two livings of Addingham and
Stanwix, his income must have been about £900, a good one by the
standards of a poor diocese like Carlisle,[21] though it must be remembered that he had to pay his curates, to whom he is said to have been
'strikingly liberal'.[22]

The Chapter at Carlisle consisted of the dean and four prebendaries.
Paley played his part in capitular business, holding in succession the
posts of treasurer (1781–3), receiver-general (1783–93), and vice-dean
(1793–5).[23] He had his stall in the cathedral, and was usually to be seen
in it, even though (for he was not an early riser) he had to miss breakfast to be present at Morning Prayer.[24] His appointment to the archdeaconry and the chancellorship made him an important figure in
diocesan affairs. His first bishop, Edmund Law, was an old man (he was
eighty-four when he died in 1787) and easy going; as Paley wrote of
him, 'the modesty, or rather bashfulness, of his nature, together with
an extreme unwillingness to give pain, rendered him sometimes less firm
and efficient in the administration of authority than was requisite'.[25]
Though he paid regular visits to his diocese, he was still Master of

Peterhouse, and can hardly have kept a very firm hand on diocesan business. It is said that John Law while archdeacon had been in effect bishop,[26] and perhaps the same could be said of Paley. He knew the clergy better than his diocesan did. Bishop Law once claimed that he could tell whether the incumbent was resident in any parish, since a resident clergyman 'threw an air of civility over the parish'. 'Why,' said Paley, 'I know a great many parishes to which I could take you, and let the whole population pass in review before you, you shall not be able to tell which is the parson. I know him by certain signs which I have learned by long practice: he has usually a black silk handkerchief round his neck, and he is more greasy than any man in the parish except the butcher. And these are your men to throw an air of civility over a people.'[27]

In the last two years of Law's episcopate and under his successors Douglas and Vernon, Paley as chancellor was responsible for the conduct of the ecclesiastical courts, which then dealt with matrimonial and testamentary cases as well as with matters more closely connected with the church. The canons required a chancellor to be 'learned in the civil and ecclesiastical laws', and though he held no degree in law Paley's lifelong interest in the administration of justice made him well qualified for the office. His duties involved him in cases of clergy discipline. He made a point, says his son, of ignoring anonymous information, sifted all reports to the bottom, and made all possible efforts to save the character of any clergyman whose case came to his notice; there was only one occasion when he was obliged to take action in a flagrant case of misconduct.[28] The reference is no doubt to the case of the Revd Joseph Gilbanks, perpetual curate of Maryport, who was deprived of his living in 1794 for 'drunkenness, neglect of duty and other irregularities and vicious excesses'.[29] Though Gilbanks was the only offender who came before the court, the sermon which Paley preached at an ordination in 1781, with its warnings against drunkenness, suggests that the standard of clerical behaviour in this respect was not very high.[30]

Paley's diocesan activities did not mean that he neglected his parochial duties at Dalston. He spent the summer months there, and when resident in Carlisle rode over to his parish almost every morning. He remained a poor horseman, and his efforts at riding were as painful to watch as they were to himself; if it is true that, as Lord Lonsdale told

the diarist Farington, he once baptized a child from horseback, perhaps
it was because he doubted his ability to dismount and remount in
safety.[31] One innovation he made in his parish was the introduction of
'afternoon lectures', that is instructional sermons—in this case exposi-
tions of Scripture—at the end of Evening Prayer, which at that time
was said in the afternoon. This service, especially in scattered country
parishes, was often ill attended, and at Dalston Paley's innovation
made a striking difference to its popularity. The congregation had
consisted of a few old people living near the church; when he started
his lectures it shot up from about twelve or fifteen to over two
hundred.[32]

His ungainliness and restlessness made him an undignified figure in
church,[33] but he was an impressive preacher. In ordinary life he was free
and unreserved in his conversation and sometimes gave the impression
of taking nothing seriously; in the pulpit he was 'all solemnity, zeal
and earnestness'.[34] When at Cambridge he recommended his pupils to
make one sermon and steal five.[35] At that time a sermon was expected
to be a weighty and finished composition and Paley's advice implies no
cynicism or encouragement to idleness. Nor does the last of the three
reasons he gave for leaving Dalston mean that he was himself negligent
in writing sermons. He gave much time and thought to their composition and was seldom without two or three unfinished ones on his table.
His early sermons, if not as Meadley describes them 'verbose and florid',
were declamatory in style and 'wanted the closeness and cogency of
his later compositions'.[36] The style he eventually adopted was plain
and unrhetorical. He went to the point at once and finished when he
had no more to say. His models, according to his son, were Sherlock,
Clarke, and Hoadly.[37] To quote one who belonged to an age better
versed than the present in pulpit eloquence, one will not find in him
'the copious invention of a Barrow, the elegant terseness of an Atter-
bury or the fine touches of an Ogden. . . . Paley's excellence consisted,
not in a fruitful and creative imagination, but in a clear understanding.
He was formed, not for an impassioned orator, but for a cool, acute,
perspicacious reasoner. . . . We see before us rather a clear headed
moralist, coolly investigating truth, analysing and dissecting with skill
the subject which he takes in hand, reasoning upon it with an accuracy
which all must understand, rather than a powerful master of eloquence'.[38]

Two minor publications of Paley's show his concern for pastoral work. One was *The Clergyman's Companion in Visiting the Sick*, which he compiled from existing material while he was at Appleby. The other was *The Young Christian Instructed in Reading and the Principles of Religion, designed for the Use of the Sunday Schools in Carlisle*. This work, which made no claim to originality, gave rise to accusations of plagiarism from a Mr Robertson, author of a spelling book part of which Paley had used in his booklet. He had taken the material from a copy, without the author's name, which had been given to one of his children, and when a London publisher wanted to reprint his booklet, Paley, who now knew the authorship of the spelling book, told the publisher he must apply for Robertson's permission, and when permission was refused declined to authorize publication. Paley gained no financial benefit from his compilation, and its publication could not have harmed the sales of Robertson's book; moreover he sent a full explanation to Robertson before the latter published his complaint. The letter to the *Gentleman's Magazine* in which he explained the position is good humoured and convincing, a model reply to a critic.[39]

Until the middle of the eighteenth century Carlisle was a small, remote, and backward cathedral city. Then industry began to develop. Woollen and linen manufactures were started, and in 1761 a calico printing works was established. The population rose from 2500 in the mid-century to 10,000 at its end. Increased prosperity brought new building, and with improved roads the town lost much of its old isolation.[40] It contained a 'circle of enlightened and well-informed gentry' whose society Paley could enjoy, and there was a club to which he belonged which met for discussion on Sunday evenings.[41] Among the clergy were some men of culture and learning. When Paley first took up residence in the city, the dean was Thomas Percy, editor of *Reliques of Ancient English Poetry*, who found him 'a most intelligent and pleasing acquaintance'.[42] Bishop Douglas, who like Percy was familiar with the literary world of London and makes a number of appearances in Boswell's *Life of Johnson*, also enjoyed Paley's company.[43] A closer friend was J. D. Carlyle, a fellow of Queens' and later professor of Arabic at Cambridge and chaplain to Lord Elgin at Constantinople. On one occasion Paley was walking with Carlyle on the Cumberland coast when his companion observed him standing in silence as if struck with admiration for something he had seen. Finally he said: 'Now see, only look at the goodness of God. How happy those shrimps are.'[44] This and other such occasions gave rise to a passage in his *Natural Theology*:

> Walking by the seaside, in a calm evening, upon a sandy shore, and with an ebbing tide, I have frequently remarked the appearance of a dark cloud, or rather, very thick mist, hanging over the edge of the water, to the height perhaps, of half a yard, and of the breadth of two or three yards, stretching along the coast as far as the eye could reach and always retiring with the water. When this cloud came to be examined, it proved to be nothing else than so much space, filled with young *shrimps*, in the act of bounding into the air from the shallow margin of the water, or from the wet sand. If any motion of a mute animal could express delight, it was this: if they had meant to make signs of their happiness, they could not have done it more intelligibly. Suppose then, what I have no doubt of, each individual of this number to be in a state of positive enjoyment: what a sum, collectively, of gratification and pleasure have we here before our view.[45]

Without being a party man Paley took a keen interest in public affairs, as is shown by his engaging defence of parliamentary government on hedonistic grounds.

> For my part, and I believe it to be the case with most men who are arrived at the middle age and occupy the middle classes of life; had I all the money, which I pay in taxes to government, at liberty to lay out upon amusement and diversion, I know not whether I could make choice of any in which I could find greater pleasure than what I receive from expecting, hearing, and relating public news; reading parliamentary debates and proceedings; canvassing the political arguments, projects, predictions, and intelligence, which are conveyed by various channels, to every corner of the kingdom. These topics ... improve conversation. They render it more rational, and more innocent. They supply a substitute for drinking, gaming, scandal, and obscenity. Now the secrecy, the jealousy, the solitude, and precipitation of despotic governments, exclude all this.[46]

At Carlisle politics were dominated by the powerful Sir James Lowther, Earl of Lonsdale from 1784. At the election of 1785 his position was challenged by J. C. Curwen, and in spite of Lonsdale's attempt to swamp the electorate by enrolling nearly fifteen hundred of his dependants as freemen, Curwen was elected. Paley took no part in electioneering, but was known to support Curwen and allowed his children to wear the blue ribands which marked his supporters.[47]

He also played his part in the movement for the abolition of the slave trade.[48] In his *Moral and Political Philosophy* he wrote forcibly of the evils of the trade and of slavery itself, and, as Thomas Clarkson said, might therefore 'be considered as having been a considerable co-adjutor in interesting the mind of the public in favour of the oppressed Africans'.[49] He remained an active supporter of abolition. He was in correspondence with the committee formed in 1787 to work for the cause, and in 1789, when the opponents of abolition were making much of the large sums that would have to be paid in compensation, he sent to the Committee 'a little treatise called Arguments against the unjust Pretensions of Slave Dealers and Holders to be indemnified by pecuniary Allowances at the public Expense in case the Slave Trade be abolished'. The substance of this was communicated to the newspapers and Clarkson believed that it had some influence with members of Parliament.[50] In 1792 Paley took the chair at a meeting at Carlisle to draw up a petition to Parliament for abolition. In his speech he pointed out that the slave trade encouraged the African chiefs to make war and enslave the vanquished, and that the continuance of 'this diabolical traffic' hindered improvements of all sorts in Africa. He dwelt on the sufferings of slaves on the passage from Africa and on the West Indian plantations, and the scanty chances of any slave having justice done to him. The slave trade, he said, was 'incompatible with the natural rights of man, contrary to the principles of religion and morality, founded in extreme injustice and cause of many cruelties'. Britain should act as was right and just even if other nations did not follow her example.[51]

The year in which this meeting took place was one in which there were widespread fears of revolution. Events in France had stimulated reformers and alarmed conservatives. Burke had written his *Reflections on the French Revolution*, and this was followed by Tom Paine's *Rights of Man*, the second part of which, published in 1792, advocated the abolition of the monarchy and of the House of Lords. Working men began for the first time to meet in Corresponding Societies and to agitate for reform. Paley reacted to these events by publishing as a pamphlet a sermon he had preached at Dalston two years earlier, with the title *Reasons for Contentment addressed to the Labouring Part of the British Public*; and at the same time, to show that he had not changed his mind with the times, he reissued the section on the British Constitution from his *Moral and Political Philosophy*.

The pamphlet is a sober essay free from alarmist rhetoric. Paley argues that the labouring man can be happy, and may be happier than the wealthy man. He concludes by pointing out that no good can be gained by a violent disturbance of society; the rich would lose and the poor would not gain.

> I (God knows) could not get my livelihood by labour, nor would the labourer find any solace or enjoyment in my studies. If we were to exchange conditions tomorrow, all the effect would be, that we both should be more miserable, and the work of both would be worse done. Without debating, therefore, what might be very difficult to decide, which of our two conditions was better to begin with, one point is certain, that it is best for each to remain in his own. The change, and the only change, to be desired, is that gradual and progressive improvement of our circumstances which is the natural fruit of successful industry; when each year is something better than the last; when we are enabled to add to our little household one article after another of new comfort and conveniency, as our profits increase, as our burden becomes less; and, what is best of all, when we can afford, as our strength declines, to relax our labours or divide our cares. This may be looked forward to, and is practicable, by great numbers in a state of public order and quiet; it is absolutely impossible in any other.

Reasons for Contentment 'was not generally read and by those who read it was not very generally admired'.[52] Paley himself called it the best thing he had ever written, and Coleridge, who later had some harsh things to say of Paley, found it helpful when an undergraduate at Cambridge.[53] Dr Parr's reaction was very different. On the walls of his drawing room at Hatton were portraits of, among others, Burke and Paley. With the publication of Burke's *Reflections* and Paley's *Reasons for Contentment* they were first hung upside down and then removed.[54] While Parr regarded Paley as a renegade who had deserted the cause of reform, others thought of him as dangerously subversive. Isaac Milner, the evangelical President of Queens', who was then Dean of Carlisle, came back from a visit to his deanery with the belief that some of the gentlemen of Carlisle were disposed to favour French principles. 'I am exceedingly sorry', he wrote, 'to find that Mr Paley is as loose in politics as he is in religion. He has considerable influence in promoting this sort of work by his conversation, which has a strong tendency to destroy all subordination and bring rules of every description into contempt.' He added that Paley was very good natured, and his own stay in Carlisle had been short; otherwise they would have come to a rupture.[55] Milner must have been an obtuse man to misjudge Paley like this. Paley had always been disposed to accept and make the best of things as they were. He certainly spoke and wrote with little respect for the great, but he accepted subordination, though only as a necessary evil. 'We recommend', he wrote, 'nothing adverse to subordinations which are established and necessary; but then it should be remembered that subordination itself is an evil, being an evil to the subordinate, who are the majority, and therefore ought not to be carried a tittle beyond what the greater good, the peaceable government of the community requires.'[56]

The domestic affections which, as he pointed out in *Reasons for Contentment*, were within the reach of all, were doubtless one of the chief sources of his own happiness. His wife was 'sensible but mild and unassuming, of retired habits, of a sweet and negative disposition, but inactive through ill health'. She 'both sufficiently accorded and was sufficiently contrasted with the ardent temper, active and positive character of her husband'. And though Paley had not married for money his wife 'added much more afterwards both to his comfort and his fortune, than he either expected or inquired after at the time'.[57] He was a good husband and a good father. There is a passage in *Moral and Political Philosophy* which was evidently inspired by his experience of parenthood.

> I seem for my part to see the benevolence of the Deity more clearly in the pleasures of very young children than in anything in the world. . . . The pleasures of a healthy infant are so manifestly provided for it by another and the benevolence of the provision is so unquestionable, that every child I see at its sport affords to my mind a kind of sensible evidence of the finger of God and the disposition which directs it.[58]

The modern reader might be inclined to dismiss these reflections as those of one sheltered from his children by an ample domestic staff; in fact we find Paley as much involved in the ties of parenthood as many fathers today. When he was at Appleby he excused himself from going round to Mr Yates on the ground that he was engaged in knitting; Yates invited him to bring his knitting with him, and he came with a stocking that he was knitting for his firstborn.[59]

As his children grew up he tried to inculcate the virtues of a well-ordered family life, though with his untidiness and addiction to late hours he did not set a very good example.[60] He encouraged his daughters to go to parties in the evening, but required one of them to stay at home to rub him in the case of an attack of rheumatism; 'this', he said, 'taught them natural affection'.[61] As for his sons, he held that one of the duties of a parent was to preserve his children in the class in which they were born, and he had a theory that they should be put into the careers least dangerous to their peculiar characters.

> Thus I would make choice of a retired life for young persons addicted to licentious pleasures; of private stations for the proud and passionate; of liberal professions and a town life for the mercenary and sottish; and not, according to the general practice of parents, send dissolute youths into the army; penurious tempers to trade; or make a crafty lad an attorney; or flatter a vain and haughty temper with elevated names, or situations, or callings, to which the fashion of the world has annexed precedency and distinction.[62]

This was written when his children were quite young, or still unborn. Whether it was in accordance with his theory or not, he sent three of his sons to the university, from which one went to the bar and two into the Church. He did not, however, regard it as essential for his sons to enter a learned profession; the youngest became a farmer, and was put to manual work in order to prepare for the life.[63]

Happy as he was in his family life, at times Paley felt the need to get away. He would go to a quiet inn at Longtown on the road north from Carlisle, ask for a room to himself, and finish the work on which he was engaged, free from the distractions of the home.[64] Or he would go out fishing. 'I have been a great follower of fishing myself,' he wrote, 'and in its cheerful solitude have passed some of the happiest hours of a sufficiently happy life; but to this moment I could never trace out the source of the pleasure which it afforded me.'[65] In the portrait by Romney, painted for the benefit of John Law, a fishing rod was incongruously added at Law's request.[66]

During the years he spent in Carlisle diocese Paley was busy reading, taking notes, and writing. From the 'confused, incoherent and blotted mass' of his notes there somehow emerged the lucid and orderly chapters of his published works.[67] His first publication after leaving Cambridge was a brief essay on the Morality of the Gospel, appended to a new edition of Edmund Law's *Reflections on the Life and Character of Christ*.[68] He then began working up into a book the material which he had used for his lectures on moral philosophy. He was encouraged to write by John Law; publication was delayed because Law thought some of the opinions advanced in it were at variance with his father's,[69] but eventually Lord Ellenborough urged him to publish, and the book appeared, with a dedicatory epistle to Edmund Law, in 1785. It was published by Faulder of New Bond Street, who at first offered £250 for it, but after Paley had received an offer of £1000 from another source, raised his to the same sum.[70] As the work went through fifteen editions in Paley's lifetime it must have proved profitable for publisher as well as author. The *Principles of Moral and Political Philosophy*, to give it its full title, was followed in 1790 by *Horae Paulinae*, in which, as the sub-title puts it, 'the truth of the Scripture history of St Paul' is 'evinced by a comparison of the Epistles which bear his name with the Acts of the Apostles and with one another', and in 1794 by *A View of the Evidences of Christianity*. These two books derived to some extent from his Cambridge teaching, but most of the work for them seems to have been done later.[71] *Horae Paulinae* was the least successful of his works so far as sales went; the *Evidences* however was immensely popular, and the first edition was sold out in a day.[72]

Promotion in the eighteenth-century Church was often the result of influence and family connections, but learning and theological writing were also rewarded, and though Paley did not, as some of the clergy did, publish in order to gain preferment, it was not unreasonable to expect that his publications would be so recognized. His *Moral and Political Philosophy*, however, was of doubtful service in this respect. There was a notorious passage which, though it was followed by a defence of property, might well in itself be thought subversive.

If you should see a flock of pigeons in a field of corn: and if instead of each picking where, and what it liked (taking just as much as it wanted, and no more) you should see ninety-nine of them gathering all they got into a heap; reserving nothing for themselves, but the chaff and the refuse; keeping this heap for one, and that the weakest, perhaps worst pigeon of the flock; sitting round, and looking on all the winter, whilst this one was devouring, throwing about and wasting it; and, if a pigeon more hardy and hungry than the rest, touched a grain of the hoard, all the others instantly flying upon it, and tearing it to pieces: if you should see this, you would see nothing more than what is practised and established among men. Among men you see the ninety and nine, toiling and scraping together a heap of superfluities for one; (and this one too, oftentimes the feeblest and worst of the whole set, a child, a woman, a madman, or a fool;) getting nothing for themselves the while, but a little of the coarsest of the provision, which their own industry produces; looking quietly on, while they see the fruits of all their labour spent or spoiled; and if one of the number take or touch a particle of the hoard, the others joining against him, and hanging him for the theft.[73]

When Paley was about to publish the book John Law said to him: 'That passage about the pigeons will not go down; it may prevent your becoming a bishop.' To which Paley replied, 'Bishop or no bishop, it shall stand.'[74]

In spite of the pigeons, in 1789, before his other books were published, Paley was offered the mastership of Jesus College, Cambridge, by the Bishop of Ely, and had reason to believe that the post would lead to the episcopate. He refused. There was no financial incentive to acceptance; the mastership was poorly paid, and Paley was not the only one to refuse it on that occasion.[75] Writing to his father, he confessed to being in a quandary. On the one hand there was the prospect of higher preferment. 'On the other hand to leave a situation with which I am much satisfied and in which I am perfectly at ease in my circumstances is a serious sort of change. I think it will end in declining it.'[76] When John Law heard of the refusal he remarked that Paley had missed a mitre.[77]

He also missed being involved with his old pupil Frend, now a

Fellow of Jesus. In 1793 Frend published his pamphlet *Peace and Union recommended to the Associated Bodies of Republicans and Anti-Republicans*. It was a time when the anti-Jacobin reaction was at its height, and the university authorities took fright at Frend's anti-clericalism and his advocacy of political reform. He was put on trial before the Vice-Chancellor, Isaac Milner, and sentenced to expulsion from the university. His expulsion from Jesus, where he had already lost his tutorship because of his avowed Unitarianism, followed. How Paley would have handled the situation, how he would have reconciled his position as head of Frend's college with his natural tolerance and fairmindedness (there was much to criticize in the conduct of the trial) is a matter of speculation.

Isaac Milner, as well as being President of Queens' and, at the time of Frend's trial, Vice-Chancellor, was from 1792 Dean of Carlisle. When the deanery became vacant Paley was generally considered a likely choice for the post, but thanks to the influence of Bishop Prety-man, Pitt's former tutor, and perhaps also to that of Wilberforce, it went to Milner.[78] Whether Paley expected, as he well might have, to get the deanery or not, he felt no resentment, and seems to have been genuinely pleased at Milner's appointment. He wrote to congratulate him, and his son recalls how he came into his house one day delighted at the news of the new dean.[79] Paley was no Evangelical, but he acknowledged that Milner was a powerful preacher and an able expo-nent of his religious position.[80]

'That such a man', wrote Meadley, '... was not advanced to a bishopric will ever remain an indelible blot on the character of those who dispensed the honours of the British hierarchy during his latter years.'[81] If he had Pitt in mind it is doubtful whether his censure was justified. It was commonly believed that Pitt wanted Paley made a bishop but that opposition came from George III, who disapproved of the sentiments of his *Moral and Political Philosophy*. The King was said to have objected to the passage about the pigeons, to Paley's opinions on the Sabbath, to the chapter on toleration, or to his com-parison of the divine right of kings to the divine right of constables;[82] and to have met Pitt's recommendation with 'What? Pigeon Paley?' or 'Not orthodox, not orthodox.'[83] Edmund Paley believed that Pitt had never put forward his father's name, but the evidence on the other side seems strong.[84] On the other hand, if George III disliked Paley's moral philosophy, he certainly thought well of him after the publication of the *Evidences*. There is a letter from an unnamed correspondent, written in 1797, describing a scene in the Chapter House of St George's Windsor. The King asks one of the canons who has taken 'my Paley' (presumably the *Evidences*) out of the library and says, 'I value the work, and would not be without it on any account.'[85] In 1799 Bishop Hurd recommended Paley, not very warmly, to the King as a possible bishop, observing that he had changed his opinions on some points since his *Moral Philosophy*,[86] and whether on this or on some other occasion George III is said to have said: 'I had rather have a man who had never had occasion to change them.' Edmund Paley records that there was an understanding in the family, 'though almost too indistinct to be now traced to any authority', that some overtures were made to his father by a friend with a view to his explaining or softening or perhaps recanting some expressions which might make against him in a higher quarter. Paley expressed himself perfectly willing to give any explanation but not disposed to recant or explain away. In 1802 there was a rumour that he was to be made Bishop of Gloucester, but no offer came. Paley did not mind.[87]

He had no reason to be dissatisfied with the rewards that followed the publication of his *Evidences*. Three bishops showed their appreciation of his work. Porteus of London presented him in 1794 to the prebend of Pancratius, or St Pancras, in St Paul's Cathedral, and shortly afterwards Pretyman of Lincoln presented him to the sub-deanery of his cathedral. He was installed there in January 1795, and from Lincoln he went to Cambridge to qualify for the degree of D.D. While at Cambridge he received a letter from the third bishop, Shute Barrington of Durham, offering him the rectory of Bishop Wearmouth. 'I really think, Betty,' he wrote to his sister, 'the bishops are bewitched.' He described how on receipt of the Bishop of Durham's letter he had set off at once to London to see him, and added: 'Lord help us in this changeable world! I don't dislike moderate bustle, but this is immoderate.'[88]

The prebend of St Paul's was a sinecure, worth about £150, not including fines (sums paid for the renewal of leases) 'of which it was not wholly unproductive'.[89] The two other benefices required residence, and Paley now left Carlisle; he vacated his prebend there, the chancellorship, and the livings of Stanwix and Addingham, but kept the archdeaconry until 1804, the year before his death. He prepared for his new life by taking a second wife. His first had died in 1791 at the age of forty after bearing ten children, two of whom died in infancy.[90] On 14 December, 1795, he married Catherine Dobinson of Carlisle. She was aged forty-six or forty-seven and the marriage was presumably dictated more by prudence than by passion. As he himself put it 'experience and reflection had convinced him that his happiness and that of his family would be greatly promoted by a union with a sensible and discerning woman'.[91]

✣4✣
Last Years

Bishop Wearmouth stands on the south side of the river Wear, opposite to Monkwearmouth, to which it was joined by a bridge in 1796.
Today both places are absorbed in Sunderland, which was already a
flourishing port and shipbuilding town in Paley's day. A separate
parish of Sunderland had been formed in 1719, but much of the new
development was in Bishop Wearmouth parish, which had a population of between nine and ten thousand. It was one of the most valuable
livings in the country, with an income, derived from tithe and glebe,
of over £1000. The rectory house, begun after the Restoration and
completed in the early eighteenth century, was large, handsome, and
in good repair.[1] 'And such a house,' wrote Paley on his appointment.
'I was told at Durham that it is one of the best parsonages in England;
and that there are not more than three bishops that have better. There
is not a shilling to be laid out upon it, and you might have rubbed it
from top to bottom with a white handkerchief without soiling it.'
The grounds and gardens were equally good, with nearly a mile of
wall planted with fruit trees, a field of ten acres, a garden shrubbery,
two or three hot-houses, and a green-house.[2]

When Paley was appointed the tithes were let for £600, but their
value in the three preceding years was £750, and Paley let them at £700
for the period of his incumbency. When there was a bad crop he could
say, with blunt north-country humour, 'Aye, aye, now I am well off;
my tithes are safe, and I have nothing to do with them, or to think about
them.'[3] In fact the arrangement was satisfactory to the lessees. It was a
period of rising agricultural prices, and they must have done well out
of the bargain. In the same way he granted long leases of his glebe,
which included a limestone quarry, on terms advantageous to the
tenants.[4] In his *Moral and Political Philosophy* he had expressed himself forcibly against the system of tithes, condemning it as a tax on
industry harmful to improvement since the titheowner shared in the

produce without having contributed anything to the production.[5] The system also had the disadvantage that the tithepayer could make things very unpleasant for the titheowner. Paley could not of course alter the system. The arrangement he made at least ensured peace and relieved him of one of the vexations of clerical life.

Today the ecclesiastical glories of Bishop Wearmouth have departed. In the nineteenth century much of the income of the benefice was relinquished to support daughter churches. The rectory and its grounds were sold for urban development, and the church has been altered out of all recognition since Paley's day. He has not, however, been entirely forgotten in his old parish. There is a Paley Street on the site of the rectory grounds, and in the church is a brass tablet to his memory erected a hundred years after his appointment to the living.

As rector of a large parish Paley was inevitably something of a public figure. He served as Justice of the Peace, and in that capacity was thought by some to be 'hasty and irascible'.[6] He left much of the parochial work to his curate, whom he treated with great respect. For a time he preached regularly, but in December 1800 he began to suffer from a painful complaint which forced him to give up both preaching and reading the services. He continued, however, to write sermons. His intention was to print a volume to be distributed free of charge to his parishioners, as they could not hear him in person; he was unable to complete this project in his lifetime, but left directions for it to be done in a codicil to his will.[7] According to his son he did 'what could reasonably be expected of any incumbent in so large a parish',[8] which was probably not a great deal by Victorian standards. It was, however, of some significance that he encouraged the existing Charity and Sunday schools at a time when some people had taken fright at the spread of revolutionary ideas and were maintaining that it was dangerous to educate the children of the poor. In 1802, when he conducted a visitation at Carlisle in place of his successor as chancellor, Professor Carlyle, he took the opportunity to refute this view, which, he said, 'insinuates that the bulk of mankind can only be governed by suppression and debasement of the intellectual faculties; and ... that the institutions of civil life rest for their support upon the ignorance of the greatest part of those who live under them'.[9]

Nonconformity flourished in his parish, and he was not worried about its popularity. He did not make the mistake of George Crabbe who, when he returned to his parish after a prolonged absence and found the Methodists established there, preached against them with a warmth which 'only irritated himself and others without bringing back disciples to the fold'.[10] Paley welcomed the activities of the Nonconformists. 'Looking at the population of this parish,' he said, 'and the smallness of your congregation at church, which, if it was filled, would not hold one-third of the parish, what must become of them if they were not in some way connected with religious persons and religious concerns?'[11]

During this last period of his life Britain was at war. When he was appointed to Bishop Wearmouth the Low Countries had been lost and the allied coalition was breaking up; three years later Ireland was in rebellion. He lived to see war renewed after the Peace of Amiens and its end was still a long way ahead when he died. He took the lead in those beneficent activities which the distress of wartime calls forth in English people. He preached on behalf of the French émigré clergy, some of whom were given shelter in the barracks at Monkwearmouth; he conversed with them as best he could through their only common language, Latin, and gave them vegetables from his garden. When food was scarce in 1799 and the well-to-do decided to help by denying themselves luxuries, he drew up the regulations to guide them.[12] At the time of the invasion threat in 1803 he intervened successfully on behalf of a young man suspected of being a spy. The general in command in the neighbourhood applied to him for a warrant to arrest the man; Paley refused, and the next day invited the suspect to a conference with the general, at which his conduct was satisfactorily explained, after which Paley helped him with money and other assistance.[13] He was not the man to be carried away by war fever. When a speaker called the French 'our atrocious and implacable enemy' he demurred. 'They have a right to come,' he said, 'and we have the right to knock 'em on the head: there is nothing atrocious in that: it is fair in war. We have done them as much harm as we could, wherever we could: they have a right to serve us the same sauce.'[14] His style in the pulpit was naturally rather different. In a sermon delivered at Durham he deserted his usual matter-of-fact manner in a concluding passage which shows that he was not oblivious of the gravity of the situation facing his country.

If ever there was a time when that steadfastness of mind, which ought to result from the study and contemplation of divine subjects, is more wanted than at another, it is the present. It is our lot to live in a distracted and eventful period. During the concussions which have shaken, and are yet shaking, the social edifice to its foundations; in the fate which we have seen of everything man calls great, of power, of wealth, and splendour—where shall thought find refuge, except in the prospects which Christianity unfolds, and in a well-grounded confidence that Christianity is true? And this support will not fail us. Erect amidst the ruins of a tottering age, the pilgrim proceeds in his course, without perturbation or dismay, endeavouring, indeed, according to his power, and interceding earnestly, for the peace and welfare of a world through which he is but directing his constant eye to a more abiding city,—to that country beyond the great river, to which the sojourning tribes are bound, and where there remaineth rest for the people of God.[15]

This sermon was preached at Durham at one of the Bishop's visitations. The bishop, Shute Barrington, was the son of a peer and the brother of a Chancellor of Exchequer, and his promotion in the Church had consequently been easy and rapid. None the less he was a good and conscientious bishop, and Paley could write sincerely of his 'earnest, active, and unwearied solicitude for the advancement of substantial Christianity'.[16] When he visited the episcopal palace at Bishop Auckland, Paley was not overawed by the dignity and high rank of the Bishop, and his simplicity and frankness contrasted with the obsequiousness of some guests. On one occasion the Bishop's wife was discoursing on the happiness of a married couple whose days were passed in complete harmony. While all the other guests expressed their admiration for this enviable life Paley remained silent. Finally when Mrs Barrington asked him what he thought about it, all he said was: 'Mighty flat, madam.'[17]

Sunderland was not a place which offered much in the way of intellectual or cultivated society, but Paley made one good friend there in G. W. Meadley, a banker and merchant of liberal views, who afterwards wrote his life. There was also an old Quaker gentleman whom he often invited to his house, and he would receive visits from friends, such as John Law, and from people who came to see him, so he said, as one of the curiosities of the place.[18] He also liked to converse with the working men of the port, ship's carpenters, rope makers, sail makers, coal heavers, and fishermen, and to question them about their life and work.[19] He was particularly interested in the new iron bridge which crossed the Wear just beyond the grounds of his rectory. This bridge, which had a span more than twice that of the pioneer iron bridge at Coalbrookdale, had an interesting history. It was originally designed by Tom Paine, and was fitted up on Paddington Green and exhibited to the public at a shilling a head. When Paine left for France, it was bought and erected over the Wear to a modified design by the architect Thomas Wilson.[20] Paley made Wilson's acquaintance, and was taken by him to the workshop, where he carefully examined every pin and screw with which it was put together.[21]

He was also able to satisfy his curiosity vicariously through his friend Carlyle. Before he set out for the East with Lord Elgin, Paley wrote to him making a series of requests for information which the professor did his best to satisfy in letters and in conversation after his return. Paley's letter, written in May 1799, is dated 'from a little Ale-house upon our road'.

He begins with prophecies, which were not in fact fulfilled, of the ecclesiastical rewards that would follow his friend's expedition. 'It is a dead hit at a Crown prebend. They can't do less *ex debito iustitiae*, as much more as they like, but I think it can't fail; so also thinks ——, who is a deep rooter. It will also be followed by some handsome marks of notice from all or some of the triumvirate of bishops.[22] This consolation awaits you if you should come home circumcised or should get into the Seven Towers.' After promising to do Carlyle's visitation for him in his absence he goes on to give a list of 'Observanda'.

1. Compare everything with English and Cumberland scenery; e.g., rivers with Eden, groves with Corby, mountains with Skiddaw. Your sensations of buildings, streets, persons, etc., etc.; e.g., whether the mufti be like Dr ——, the grand seignior, Mr ——, etc.

2. Give us one day at Constantinople minutely from morning to night; what you do, see, eat, and hear.

3. Let us know what the common people have to dinner; get, if you can, a peasant's actual dinner and bottle: for instance, if you see a

man working in the fields, call to him to bring the dinner he has with him, and describe it minutely.

4. Their little-houses—I reckon much upon them—'drawing', as Tristram Shandy says, 'men's characters from their evacuations'; and no author has written upon the subject fully enough!

5. The diversions of the common people. Whether they seem to enjoy their amusements, and be happy, and sport and laugh. Farm-houses, or anything answering to them, and of what kind, same of public-houses, roads.

6. Their shops. How you get your breeches mended, or things done for you, and how, i.e., well or ill done. Whether you see the tailor, converse with him, etc., etc.

7. Get into the inside of a cottage, describe furniture, utensils, what you actually find doing.

All the stipulation I make with you for doing your visitation is, that you come over to Wearmouth soon after your return, for you will be very entertaining—between truth and lying. I have a notion you will find books, but in great confusion as to catalogues, classing etc., etc.

8. Describe minutely how you pass one day on shipboard. Learn to take and apply lunar or other observations, and how the mid-shipmen, etc., etc. do it.

9. What sort of fish you get, and how dressed.

I should think your business would be to make yourself master of the middle Greek. My compliments to Buonaparte, if you meet with him, which I think is very likely. Pick up little articles of dress, tools, furniture, especially from low life; as an actual smock, etc., etc.

10. What they talk about—company.

11. Describe your impression upon first seeing things, upon catching the first view of Constantinople—the novelties of the first day you pass there.

In all countries and climates, nations, and languages, carry with you the best wishes of, my dear Carlyle,

Your affectionate friend
W. Paley[23]

In the home Paley followed a fixed routine. He allotted one hour to breakfast, one to dinner and the newspaper, one in the evening to light reading, and two separate periods of an hour to the garden. Walking round the garden with his youngest daughter he was usually silent, but now and then burst into laughter or recited scraps of poetry or prose.

> With the handle of his stick in his mouth, now moving in a short hurried step, now stopping at a butterfly, a flower, a snail, etc.; at one instant pausing to consider the subject of his next sermon, at the next carrying the whole weight and intent of his mind to the arranging some pots in his green-house, or preparing with the greatest gravity to remove some stick or stand that offended his eye, he presented the most prominent feature of his mind very obviously, but made it perhaps happy for his public character that he chose to be alone.[24]

He continued to study and to write. He now set to work seriously on a subject that he had already had in mind when at Carlisle, the subject of his last book, *Natural Theology*, which he published in 1802.[25] He read widely, and he studied the works of nature to find material for his work. The bones of a hare, fowl, or fish would be taken from the dinner table to the study to be examined for evidences of the contrivances of the beneficent creator, the divine architect who had made, for instance, the hare's backbone on just the same principle as that followed in the design of the bridge over the Wear.[26]

From Bishop Wearmouth we turn to Lincoln. The subdeanery which Paley held there was worth about £700 a year, with the prospect of an additional sum from fines, and carried with it a large, indeed inconveniently large house.[27] 'Formerly', said Paley, 'the Dean of Lincoln had so much to do that he was obliged to have a subdean to help him; but now I cannot find out for the life of me that there is anything for either of us to do.'[28] In fact the subdean had as much, or as little, to do as other cathedral residentiaries. At Lincoln the dean, subdean, chancellor, and precentor shared the cathedral duties. Each had three months of residence, the subdean taking the first quarter of each year, though Paley used to stay on after the end of his residence until the beginning of May.[29] He was also by virtue of his office Master of Trinity Hospital, West Retford, and he took an active interest in its affairs. He discovered that the bailiff of the estate with which the hospital was endowed was also tenant of one of its farms; conscious of the abuses likely to arise from such a situation and finding that the bailiff had been appointed without consultation with the governors he took the case to the Chancery Court, which decided in his favour.[30]

While his home life was centred in Bishop Wearmouth, at Lincoln he was more of a figure in society. He belonged to a literary society whose meetings ended with oysters and a rubber of his favourite whist.[31] He entertained and he dined out. Everyone liked him, though some thought him lacking in the dignity which befitted a man of his position. 'The familiarity of his manners, his almost perpetual jests, his approximations to coarseness of language, weakened the splendour of his literary reputation by which we should otherwise have been dazzled.'[32] He was 'a thick, short, square-built man, with a face which though animated and cheerful, could not but, at first sight, appear ugly; with bushy brows, snub nose and projecting teeth; with an awkward gait and movement of the arms; a decent and dignified but by no means excessive protuberance of the belly; wearing a white wig'. He refused to wear the apron, or short cassock, then thought the proper garb for dignitaries of the church, saying that it was like the aprons worn by tailors in Durham.[33] He drank little, but was fond of his food and made no secret of it. 'Mr Subdean, what will you be pleased to eat?' asked his hostess. 'Eat, madam? Eat anything, from the top of the table to the bottom, from the beginning of the first course to the end of the second.' Then, after a pause during which he put on an air of grave deliberation, 'There are those pork steaks. I had intended to proceed regularly and systematically, through the ham and fowls to the beef; but those pork steaks stagger my system.'[34]

He had a fund of anecdotes, delivered 'with a peculiarly animated countenance and a characteristic curling of the nose'.[35] His variety of voice and facial expression made even the most ordinary remarks seem amusing. He liked to tell stories against himself, to deflate pretensions, and to act the blunt northcountryman. At times he would indulge in nonsense like the following.

I have often thought that if I was to turn swindler, I would try to swindle in the character of a dignified ecclesiastic. It would be quite a new thing, and nobody would suspect it. Bishops, however, are too well known: it would not be safe to pretend to be a bishop. Even an English dean might appear *in propria persona* and push one out of one's place; but an Irish dean, ay, that would do very well: even the titles of Irish deans are, many of them, unknown in England; for example, the Dean of Aghadoe. Well, I would take a good house at the end of the town, or in Marybone, and I would have a fine brass plate on my door, on which should be inscribed, in grand uncial letters, 'Dean of Aghadoe'. Then I would wear a short cassock—nothing to be done without a black apron. So I would begin to run into debt: nobody would refuse to trust the Dean of Aghadoe: I would order in goods—every sort of thing that could be easily disposed of, and before I had exhausted my credit, before anyone began to suspect, I would be off, and the Dean of Aghadoe would be returned *non inventus*.[36]

Paley's jesting might seen undignified and out of keeping with his clerical character, but it could serve a useful purpose. A French émigré priest had settled in Lincoln, where he gave lessons in French, and Paley used to entertain him, more out of kindness than because he found him congenial. One of the Lincoln clergy, Henry Best, had joined the Church of Rome, and the priest was blamed for this and for other proselytizing activities. When Paley heard of these accusations he said: '*He* convert anyone! He never converted anything in his life, except a neck of mutton into chops.' After that nothing more was heard of these suspicions and the priest was left in peace.[37]

Paley always maintained that God intended man to be happy in this world, and he lived up to his belief. He had been happy in earlier life, but he now decided that there was more happiness in old age than in youth. 'The young', he wrote, 'are not happy but when enjoying happiness; the old are happy when free from pain. And this constitution suits with the degree of animal power which they respectively possess. The vigour of youth was to be stimulated to action by impatience of rest; whilst to the imbecility of age, quietness and repose become positive gratifications. In one important respect the advantage is with the old. A state of ease is, generally speaking, more attainable than a state of pleasure.'[38] Even sickness and pain did not shake his belief. In 1800 he was attacked by what is described as 'a violent nephralgic complaint accompanied with a species of melaena'.[39]

In the winter of 1801–2 he had another attack, and in the following May, on the advice of his doctor, he went to Buxton to take the waters. He was finishing his *Natural Theology* and his doctor, who was also at Buxton, was much impressed by the way in which he bore his pain and cheerfully resumed his writing as soon as it passed off.[40] He was writing his chapter 'Of the Goodness of the Deity', and while his own experiences were fresh in his mind he included the following passage:

> Pain ... may be violent and frequent; but it is seldom both violent and long continued: and its pauses and intermissions become positive pleasures. It has the power of shedding a satisfaction over intervals of ease, which, I believe, few enjoyments exceed. .... I am far from being sure, that a man is not a gainer by suffering a moderate interruption of bodily ease for a couple of hours out of the four-and-twenty. Two very common observations favour this opinion: one is, that remissions of pain call forth, from those who experience them, stronger expressions of satisfaction and of gratitude towards both the author and the instruments of their relief than are excited by advantages of any other kind: the second is, that the spirits of sick men do not sink in proportion to the acuteness of their sufferings; but rather appear to be roused and supported, not by pain, but by the high degree of comfort which they derive from its cessation, or even its subsidency whenever that occurs; and which they taste with a relish, that diffuses some portion of mental complacency over the whole of that mixed state of sensations in which disease has placed them.[41]

He went on to write of the value of disease in abating or even extinguishing the horror of death, and in his final chapter he considered the future state after death. His book ends with the words: 'Upon the whole; in everything which respects this awful, but, as we trust, glorious change, we have a wise and powerful Being (the author, in nature, of infinitely various expedients for infinitely various ends), upon whom to rely for the choice and appointment of means, adequate to the execution of any plan which his goodness or his justice may have formed, for the moral and accountable part of his terrestrial creation. That great office remains with him: be it ours to hope and prepare, under a firm and settled persuasion, that, living and dying, we are with him; that life is passed in his constant presence, that death resigns us to his merciful disposal.' He was prepared for the end when it came three years later. A writer in the *Quarterly Review* compared him to Socrates and applied to him the closing words of the *Phaedo* in which Plato called his master the best, wisest, and justest of men.[42] Another Greek philosopher comes to mind, Epicurus, who, though he did not share Paley's belief in a beneficent providence and in a future life, like him believed in man's capacity for happiness, observed that pain if acute did not last long, and remained serene and happy even in his painful last illness.

Paley was buried in Carlisle cathedral. The brass on his tombstone in the north choir aisle reads: 'Here lie interred the remains of Wm Paley D.D. who died May 15, 1805 Aged 62 years', and a mural tablet at the east end of the choir adds that he was archdeacon and chancellor of the diocese. These simple inscriptions are well suited to his straightforward and unaffected character.

5

Moral Philosophy

Paley's *Moral and Political Philosophy* belongs to that class of treatises of which the classical example is Cicero's *De Officiis*, the aim of which is not so much to investigate the theory of ethics as to instruct in the duties of everyday life. It originated in his lectures as tutor of Christ's and should be seen in the context of the Cambridge tradition of moral philosophy teaching. Apart from *De Officiis*, which was still read, though it had lost something of the authority it once held, two widely used books were Grotius *De Iure Belli et Pacis* and Pufendorf *De Officiis Hominis et Civis iuxta Legem Naturae*, translated into English with the title *The whole Duty of Man according to the Law of Nature.* From Cambridge itself came Thomas Rutherforth's *Institutes of Natural Law* (1754–6), allegedly lectures on Grotius, but in fact an independent work bearing little relation to that of Grotius. Paley's own tutor Backhouse had used the *Introduction to Moral Philosophy* of the Glasgow professor Francis Hutcheson.[1]

Paley found all the current treatises unsatisfactory. The works of Grotius and Pufendorf were 'too much mixed up with the civil law and with the jurisprudence of Germany to answer precisely the design of a system of ethics—the direction of private consciences in the general conduct of human life'; they were (and this applied particularly to Grotius) more concerned with the relations of states than with domestic life; and they were overloaded with quotations from the classics. Modern English writers had the fault of separating the law of nature from the precepts of revelation; some, like the Scotsman Adam Ferguson in his *Institutes of Moral Philosophy*, were too inclined to enunciate a series of detached propositions without continuous argument, while others, like Rutherforth, dwelt to excess on elementary verbal distinctions. Paley's own method of proceeding was determined by the origin of the book. He had found in his college teaching that it was harder to make his pupils see the difficulty in an ethical question than to understand its solution; it was necessary therefore to put the case in such a way as to suggest doubts and excite curiosity. He had tried too to deal with real problems, with questions likely to arise in the ordinary life of his day, and on each point he combined 'the conclusions of reason with the declarations of Scripture, where they are to be had, as of co-ordinate authority'.[2]

Paley's lecture notes show that he covered much the same ground with his pupils as in his published book, though he treated his material in a different order.[3] Lecture notes, as all lecturers know, grow; they are altered and added to as the lecturer reads new books or has new ideas. Paley's were no exception. He inserted what he thought of value without recording his source, and when he wrote up his material for publication he found it impossible, or did not think it worth while, to acknowledge his debts. He did not claim to be completely original, though he did claim to be more than a compiler.

To one writer, however, he acknowledged a particular debt, Abraham Tucker. Tucker was a country gentleman with a taste for study and speculation who wrote, under the pseudonym of Edward Search, a long discursive work entitled *The Light of Nature pursued*, the first four books of which were published in 1768 and the rest posthumously in 1778. 'I have found', wrote Paley, ' in this writer more original thinking and observation upon the several subjects that he has taken in hand, than in any other, not to say than in all others put together. . . . But his thoughts are diffused through a long, various and irregular work. I shall account it no mean praise, if I have been some-times able to dispose into method, to collect into heads and articles, or to exhibit in more compact and tangible masses, what, in that otherwise excellent performance, is spread over too much surface.'[4] Paley's debt to Tucker is rather less than these words might suggest. *The Light of Nature* contains much speculation, often fanciful, on philosophical and theological questions which seems alien to Paley's forthright common-sense attitude. But he willingly accepted Tucker's general thesis, that reason and revelation support one another, that both bid us be happy, and that the good of the individual is best promoted by promoting the general good and so increasing the general stock of happiness.

Paley includes the questions regularly handled in the moral treatises of his day: property, contracts, wills, oaths, vows and promises, marriage, and the duties of parents and children; he makes use of traditional divisions such as that of duties into those towards God, towards oneself and towards others, and of rights into natural and adventitious, alienable and unalienable, perfect and imperfect. But in spite of a certain amount of traditional material his work has a strongly individual character. Its forceful style, telling illustrations, and sense of the realities of life distinguish it from other academic productions of the day. One has only to glance at the works of Ferguson, Hutcheson, or Rutherforth to recognize Paley's superiority. J. M. Keynes once described his *Moral and Political Philosophy* as an immortal book.[5] It is hardly immortal in the sense that Plato's *Republic* or Aristotle's *Ethics* are, but at least it has more life in it than some works of greater pretensions and greater repute.

After briefly considering the various rules by which men are ordinarily governed, the 'law of honour' (the code of conduct in use among men of fashion), the law of the land, and the Scriptures,[6] all of them inadequate in various ways, Paley proceeds to consider the existence of a moral sense, or instinctive perception of right and wrong. He concludes that either no instincts exist such as to form a moral sense, or that they cannot be distinguished from prejudices or habits. It is not safe to assume certain principles as dictates of nature and then draw conclusions from them as to the rightness or wrongness of actions independent of their tendency; a system of morality based on instincts will only discover reasons and excuses for opinions and practices already established.[7]

After a chapter on happiness, to which we shall return shortly, Paley goes on to define virtue. 'Virtue is "the doing good to mankind, in obedience to the will of God, and for the sake of everlasting happiness".' He proclaims his definition, says Leslie Stephen, 'as calmly as if he were giving Euclid's definition of parallel straight lines'.[8] It was not in fact, as Paley's inverted commas show, his own definition; he took it word for word from Edmund Law.[9] It did not accord with the sentiment of the nineteenth century. To say that one does good for the sake of everlasting happiness smacked of selfishness. As J. S. Mill put it, if there was one clear requirement of Christianity it was that of loving and practising good simply because it was good; and he contrasted this with Paley's view, or his own version of Paley's view, that the reason for doing good is 'that God is stronger than we are, and is able to damn us if we do not'.[10] The eighteenth century thought differently. If a man's aim was personal happiness, it was only natural that he should take account of his happiness in the next world as well as in this. A system of rewards and punishments after death was part of the teaching of Christianity and could not be ignored by the Christian; and so far from being selfish, a morality based on such a system was an encouragement to disinterested conduct which looked beyond the prospect of immediate reward. When Paley wrote, few would have been shocked or surprised at his invoking everlasting happiness as the aim of virtue.

The definition which he adopted from Law cleared up in Paley's opinion the problem of moral obligation, about which, he says, an air of mystery seemed to hang when he first turned his thoughts to moral speculations. Moral obligation, he now saw, was like all other obligations, nothing more than 'an inducement of sufficient strength, and resulting, in some way, from the command of another'. The motive was the expectation of reward after this life, the command that of God. 'This solution goes to the bottom of the subject, as no further question can reasonably be asked.' Those who rejected Christianity must form their moral system independent of the supernatural sanction, as Hume had done, but for the Christian it was impossible to ignore these considerations.[11] Yet when Bentham constructed a system of morals based solely on this world it was not very different from Paley's. 'Bentham is Paley *minus* a belief in hellfire', wrote Leslie Stephen.[12] 'Hellfire' belongs to Stephen's vocabulary rather than to Paley's, but if we substitute for it 'rewards and punishments in a future life' the epigram can stand. Paley's moral teaching might well be criticized as too much based on the values of this world.

Apart from the question of 'everlasting happiness' Law's definition of virtue is open to criticism. It limits it unduly in confining it to 'the doing good to mankind'. Paley himself wrote elsewhere of 'passive virtues' as perhaps the most acceptable to the deity, and expressed the opinion that a West Indian slave who amidst his wrongs retained his benevolence was among the foremost of human candidates for the rewards of virtue.[13] Shortly after giving Law's definition he refers to the threefold division of virtue into duty towards God, towards other men and towards ourselves, and he himself makes use of this division later in his work. Duties towards God and towards ourselves can hardly be called 'doing good to mankind.'[14] This is the sort of inconsistency that arises from accumulating notes from various sources.

If the will of God provides man with his rule, the business of morality is to discover that will. This can be found first in his express declarations, that is to say in the Scriptures, and secondly by the light of nature. Man is like an ambassador who has precise instructions from his sovereign on some points, but on others has to be guided by what he knows of the sovereign's general inclination.[15] Scripture does not give specific directions on every moral question. It lays down general rules and illustrates them by examples whether fictitious (parables) or drawn fom actual circumstances. It does not teach new rules so much as enforce morality by new sanctions and a greater certainty.[16] Paley's usual method therefore is to proceed by 'the light of nature' and to reinforce its conclusions where appropriate by the authority of revelation. In some cases, as in that of slavery, the Scriptures give us no guidance. Occasionally the light of nature fails; Paley can find few valid arguments to establish man's right to eat the flesh of animals, and has to fall back on the permission given to Noah and his family.[17] At times the precepts of Scripture seem at first sight to conflict with the rules that can be deduced from nature. 'When thou doest alms, let not thy left hand know what thy right hand doeth.' This should not be taken as enjoining universal secrecy in charitable acts—for there may be good reasons for publicity—but rather as forbidding ostentation.[18] The precept to turn the other cheek is not to be interpreted as forbidding all opposition to and defence against injury, but rather as a proverbial way of describing the general duties of forgiveness and benevolence.[19]

To discover the will of God by the light of nature we must inquire into 'the tendency of the action to promote or diminish the general happiness'. When God created the human species he provided it with the means to happiness; all the contrivances of nature are designed for beneficial purposes and not to cause pain. From this it follows that God wills the happiness of mankind.[20] 'So then actions are to be estimated by their tendency. Whatever is expedient is right. It is the utility of any moral rule alone which constitutes the obligation of it.'[21] If it is objected that there are some actions which appear to be useful but are clearly not right, the answer is that the utility is only apparent. The assassination of a wicked landowner might free the neighbourhood of a pernicious tyrant, but apart from the harm done to the man himself the action would be bad in its consequences, as it would violate the general rule that no man should be put to death for his crimes except by public authority. One must consider not only immediate consequences but those likely to ensue in the long run. Apparently trivial offences have, or would have if condoned, as serious general consequences as those which cause greater immediate harm. 'The crime and fate of the housebreaker is the same whether his booty be five pounds or fifty. And the reason is, that the general consequence is the same.'[22]

If human happiness is what God wills it is important to know in what happiness consists. Paley does not attempt, as J. S. Mill later did, to distinguish between the quality of pleasures. He declines to indulge in the 'usual declamation' on the 'worthiness, refinement, and delicacy of some satisfactions, or the meanness, grossness, and sensuality of others'.[23] He holds that pleasures differ only in continuance and intensity, and it is only on an assessment of this and observation of what conduces to cheerfulness and contentment in everyday life that we must base our ideas of human happiness.

Happiness, according to Paley, does not consist in the pleasures of food, drink, and sex, nor in more refined pleasures such as those of music and painting, nor in active sports such as hunting, shooting, and fishing. (Strange that he should have included fishing, which he himself acknowledged to be one of the chief sources of his own happiness.) These pleasures do not last for long and they lose their relish by repetition. Moreover, an eagerness for intense pleasures takes away our satisfaction in others, in 'those gently soothing engagements, the due variety and succession of which are the only things that supply a vein or continued state of happiness'. Nor does happiness consist in freedom from pain and care; such a state usually produces depression and imaginary anxieties. Finally it does not consist in greatness or elevated station. Superiority only yields satisfaction if it is obtained over those with whom we compare ourselves. The pleasures of ambition are not peculiar to high stations. 'The farrier who shoes a horse better and who is in greater request for his skill than any man within ten miles of him, possesses, for all that I can see, the delight of distinction and of excelling, as truly and substantially as the statesman, the soldier and the scholar, who have filled Europe with the reputation of their wisdom, their valour or their knowledge.' But even if the pleasures of ambition are common to all classes, it is doubtful whether they do not involve just as much pain as pleasure.

Turning from what happiness is not to what it is Paley suggests that it consists firstly in the exercise of social and domestic affections ('To the want of these may be imputed the peevishness of monks.' How many monks had Paley met?) and in acts of bounty and beneficence. Secondly it consists in 'the exercise of our faculties either of body or mind in the pursuit of some engaging end'. 'Engagement is everything: the more significant, however, our engagements are, the better: such as the planning of laws, institutions, manufactures, charities, improvements, public works; and the endeavouring, by our interest, address, solicitations, and activity, to carry them into effect: or, upon a smaller scale, the procurement of a maintenance and fortune for our families by a course of industry and application to our callings, which forms and gives motion to the common occupations of life; training up a child; prosecuting a scheme for his future establishment; making ourselves masters of a language or a science; improving or managing an estate; labouring after a piece of preferment; and, lastly, *any* engagement, which is innocent, is better than none; as the writing a book, the building of a house, the laying out of a garden, the digging of a fishpond—even the raising of a cucumber or a tulip.' Thirdly happiness depends on 'the prudent constitution of the habits', which should be such that any change from them is for the better; for example, those who are used to simple food will enjoy a feast whereas the epicure must always feed luxuriously. Finally, happiness consists in health. 'When we are in perfect health and spirits, we feel in ourselves a happiness independent of any particular outward gratification whatever, and of which we can give no account. This is an enjoyment which the Deity has annexed to life; and probably constitutes, in a great measure, the happiness of infants and brutes, especially of the lower and sedentary orders of animals, as of oysters, periwinkles and the like; for which I have sometimes been at a loss to find out amusement.' Happiness, Paley concludes, is pretty equally distributed amongst the different orders of society, and vice contributes no more to it than virtue.[25]

That the poor are, or can be, as happy as the rich, was the theme of his pamphlet *Reasons for Contentment*. In this he deprecates comparisons between our own condition and that of others. He points out that if the law protects the rich it also protects the poor and weak, and if large fortunes are an evil, the evil should be borne for the sake of the maintenance of rules which are in the interest of all. The labouring man has his regular occupation which keeps him active in body and mind; frugality is itself a pleasure, an agreeable exercise demanding attention and contrivance. The poor are free from the difficulties which the rich find in placing their children in positions suited to their expectations; 'with health of body, innocence of mind, and habits of industry, a poor man's child has nothing to be afraid of'. The poor enjoy their simple food as much as the rich enjoy their delicacies; the rich cannot enjoy the pleasure of resting after fatigue. The chief source of happiness, the exercise of the domestic affections, is as open to the poor as to the rich.[26]

The spectacle, according to De Quincey, is not a pleasant one 'of rich people such as Paley and Hannah More, sitting in luxurious saloons and lecturing their poor hardworking fellow countrymen upon the enormity of the blessings which they enjoy'.[27] 'Luxurious saloons' is hardly appropriate to Paley's untidy study, but De Quincey's reaction will probably be shared by most modern readers. In other ages his theme would have been thought a commonplace. It was a common topic of moralists in the ancient world that poverty was no ill and that man should be content with a little. Seneca observed that the poor man laughs more often than the rich and that his laugh is more genuine; St Augustine contrasted the happiness of the beggar he met in the streets of Milan with his own unhappy state at a time when he was aiming at worldly success.[28] Swift has a sermon 'On the Poor Man's Contentment', on the same lines as Paley's but without his humanity.[29] Those who have dilated on this theme have seldom been poor themselves, nor have they had much success in persuading the poor to be content with their lot. None the less it remains true that wealth does not necessarily bring happiness and that the simple pleasures which in Paley's view constitute happiness are easily attainable. Admittedly even these pleasures are hardly compatible with a life of extreme toil and want, but Paley would never have maintained that they were. He himself observed that habit can never reconcile men to the extremities of cold, hunger, and thirst any more than it can reconcile the hand to the touch of a red-hot iron, and that 'pride, or prudence, or delicacy, or love of ease, keep one half of the world out of the way of observing what the other half suffer'.[30]

God wills the happiness of his creatures and the will of God is the measure of right and wrong.[31] On the basis of these principles Paley discusses the various questions of conduct which arise in this life. He deals with such old problems of casuistry as whether promises should always be kept and whether it is ever right to tell a lie. He does not, however, waste time over cases unlikely ever to occur, such as those where moral philosophers invoked the 'law of extreme necessity' to justify, for example, saving one's own life when two shipwrecked men seize on a plank which will only support one.[32] Paley's aim was to give guidance in the situations likely to arise in contemporary life. Of these many depended on the legal and conventional arrangements of society and in particular on the institution of property.

As we have seen, Paley introduced his discussion of property with a provocative picture of a flock of pigeons collecting together all the best grain for the benefit of a single pigeon. He went on to point out that there were none the less substantial advantages in this apparently unnatural institution. It increased the produce of the earth, preserved it to maturity, prevented contests, and improved the conveniency of living.[33] He reviews the various theories which had been advanced about the origin of property and its justification, and finds them all unsatisfactory. His own theory is that 'the real foundation of our right is the law of the land'.[34] It is the will of God that the produce of the earth be applied to man's use. This involves the institution of property. The land cannot be divided into separate property without the law of the country regulating its division, and it is therefore consistent with the will of God that the law should so regulate it.[35] But it is contrary to the will of God and therefore wrong to waste or misapply the produce of the earth. 'Schemes of wealth or profit, prompt the active part of mankind to cast about, how they may convert their property to the most advantage: and their own advantage, and that of the public, commonly concur. But it has not yet entered into the minds of mankind, to reflect that it is a *duty*, to add what we can to the common stock of provision, by extracting out of our estates the most they will yield; or that it is any sin to neglect this.'[36]

Though many of the duties of life are determined by the law of the land, there remain important ones which are not, and which provide greater scope for the exercise of virtue. Chief among these is the obligation of charity, which Paley, in accordance with his general ethical theory, defines as 'the promoting the happiness of our inferiors'.[37] Among these inferiors are servants and other dependants. When a party of friends, says Paley, are on a journey and find it best for all to divide up the duties between themselves, the one who assumes direction of the party does not forget that all were equal when they set out and are to return to a level again at their journey's end, and treats all with the same consideration; we should act in the same way towards those who 'in the casting of the parts of human society, happen to be placed within our power'. And he adds a point which some of his contemporaries might have found it hard to accept. Our obligation to our dependants is much greater than theirs to us. It is not correct to say that the rich man maintains his servants, tradesmen, tenants, and labourers; they maintain him. Their industry provides him with good clothes and amusement; it is not the estate but the labour on it that pays his rent. Nor does Paley find any foundation for the opinion often expressed that good treatment is wasted on 'low and ordinary minds'. 'If by "low and ordinary minds" are meant the minds of men in low and ordinary stations, they seem to be affected by benefits in the same way that all others are, and to be no less ready to requite them: and it would be a very unaccountable law of nature if it were otherwise.'[38]

Among dependants slaves occupied a special position. Paley can only condemn the whole institution in the strongest terms. As we have seen, he was a consistent opponent both of the slave trade and of slavery itself. He acknowledges that English slave-owners were especially brutal, and poses the question, now that the American colonies had been lost, 'whether a legislature which had so long lent its assistance to the support of an institution replete with human misery, was fit to be trusted with an empire the most extensive that ever obtained in any age or quarter of the world'.[39]

The relief of the poor is 'a remedy for those inequalities and distresses which God foresaw that many must be exposed to under every general rule for the distribution of property'. The division of property was allowed on condition that everyone had enough for subsistence, and since this cannot be guaranteed by any regulation of property, voluntary bounty must come into operation. Of the various ways in which it can be exercised the least satisfactory is the relief of beggars, but Paley does not endorse the view that on this account all begging appeals should be rejected. We must consider not only the effect on the beggar but also that on ourselves; if we resolve to deny our humanity in this way we shall end up by losing our humanity altogether.[40]

The principle of the general happiness is invoked in support of the institution of marriage.[41] This serves 'the private comfort of individuals especially of the female sex', and those who are not affected by this consideration should remember that what promotes the happiness of the majority is binding upon the whole. Marriage also ensures the production of healthy children and their education and settlement in life; it promotes peace in society by assigning one woman to one man; it supports civil authority by the authority of the parent and provides the state with additional security for the good behaviour of its citizens; finally it encourages industry. With regard to divorce the only principle applicable is that of general expediency, and this points to the indissolubility of marriage. If the two parties know that they must live together till death, they will take pains to give up what offends and practise what pleases the other.

> A man and woman in love with one another will do this insensibly; but love is neither general nor durable; and where that is wanting, no lessons of duty, no delicacy of sentiment, will go half so far with the generality of mankind and womankind as this one intelligible reflection, that they must make the best of their bargain, and seeing that they must either both be miserable or both share in the same happiness, neither can find their own comfort but in promoting the pleasure of the other.[42]

Moreover, divorce operates on the whole to the disadvantage of the woman, 'and the only question appears to be, whether the real and permanent happiness of one half of the species should be surrendered to the caprice and voluptuousness of the other'.[43]

Having established the advantages of marriage, Paley argues against sexual relations outside marriage primarily on the ground that they weaken the institution and defeat the beneficial purposes for which it is designed. And if fornication is criminal, we must consider as accessories to the crime all incentives to it, such as 'wanton songs, pictures, books; the writing, publishing, and circulating of which, whether out of frolic, or for some pitiful profit, is productive of so extensive a mischief from so mean a temptation, that few crimes, within the reach of private wickedness, have more to answer for, or less to plead in their excuse'.[44]

When he comes to the duties of parents Paley appears, as he does elsewhere in his work, more as the practical moralist than as the moral philosopher. The following passage shows him in this role:

Parents, to do them justice, are seldom sparing in lessons of virtue and religion; in admonitions which cost little, and which profit less; whilst their *example* exhibits a continual contradiction of what they teach. A father, for instance, will, with much solemnity and apparent earnestness, warn his son against idleness, excess in drinking, debauchery, and extravagance, who himself loiters about all day without employment; comes home every night drunk; is made infamous in his neighbourhood by some profligate connection; and wastes the fortune which should support, or remain a provision for his family, in riot or luxury or ostentation. Or he will discourse gravely before his children of the obligation and importance of revealed religion, whilst they see the most frivolous and oftentimes feigned excuses detain him from its reasonable and solemn ordinances. Or he will set before him, perhaps, the supreme and tremendous authority of Almighty God; that such a being ought not to be named, or even thought upon, without sentiments of profound awe and veneration. This may be the lecture he delivers to his family one hour; when the next, if an occasion arise to excite his anger, his mirth, or his surprise, they will hear him treat the name of the Deity with the most irreverent profanation, and sport with the terms and denunciations of the Christian religion, as if they were the language of some ridiculous and long-exploded superstition. Now even a child is not to be imposed upon by such mockery. He sees through the grimace of this counterfeit concern for virtue. He discovers that his parent is acting a part; and receives his admonitions as he would hear the same maxims from the mouth of a player. . . .

A good parent's first care is to be virtuous himself: his second, to make his virtues as easy and engaging to those about him as their nature will admit. Virtue itself offends, when coupled with forbidding manners. And some virtues may be urged to such excess, or brought forward so unseasonably, as to discourage and repel those who observe and who are acted upon by them, instead of exciting an inclination to imitate and adopt them. Young minds are particularly liable to these unfortunate impressions. For instance, if a father's oeconomy degenerate into a minute and teasing parsimony, it is odds but that the son, who has suffered under it, set out a sworn enemy to all rules of order and frugality. If a father's piety be morose, rigorous, and tinged with melancholy, perpetually breaking in upon the recreation of his family, and surfeiting them with the language of religion upon all occasions, there is danger lest a son carry from home with him a settled prejudice against seriousness and religion, as inconsistent with every plan of a pleasurable life, and turn out, when he mixes with the world, a character of levity and dissoluteness.[45]

Paley's chapters on duties towards God belong rather to religion than to moral philosophy and will be considered in a later chapter. Under duties to ourselves he treats of the right of self-defence, drunkenness, and suicide. He points out that in fact there are few duties which do not also involve other people, and even in the case of drunkenness and suicide he takes into account their social implications. Apart from the ill effects of drunkenness on the drunkard himself it sets a bad example. It has a way of spreading, and though a particular individual may suffer little from it, others whom he influences will suffer. It is a vice, he says, which usually meets with milder names and more indulgence than it deserves.[46] In the case of suicide Paley insists on the importance of considering general consequences. There may be individual cases, as there are of murder, where the guilt is not easily established, but the essential question is the general one, whether everyone who chooses to take his life may do so; and if this was admitted, it would mean the loss of many potentially useful lives and pain on the part of those bereaved.[47] Apart from this, as he argues elsewhere, a man contemplating suicide may doubt whether it is lawful to destroy himself, but he can have no doubt that it is lawful not to; on doubtful points we are bound to take the safe side.[48]

In his notes on the Morality of the Gospel published as an appendix to Law's *Reflections on the Life and Character of Christ*, and dating from his Cambridge days, Paley's approach is rather different from that of his *Moral Philosophy*. Though he asserts that the morality of the gospel is not beyond what might be discovered by reason, he is concerned to show its difference from, and superiority to, that of contemporary Judaea and of the Greek and Roman philosophers. Curiously enough he seems to repudiate the fundamental doctrine of his *Moral Philosophy*. 'The gospel maxims', he writes, ' "loving our neighbour as ourselves and doing as we would be done by" are much superior rules of life to the το πρεπον of the Greek or the *honestum* of the Roman moralists, in forming ideas of which, people put in or left out just what they pleased; and better than the *utile* or *general expediency* of the modern, which few can estimate.' Utility or general expediency is the basis of Paley's own moral theory. Though one should not perhaps put too much weight on a brief sentence in what, although published, remained only notes, there certainly seems to be some discrepancy here.[49]

In 1776, the same year in which these notes were published, appeared a short work entitled *A View of the Internal Evidence of the Christian Religion* by Soame Jenyns, a miscellaneous writer who had been an unbeliever, but became convinced of the truth of Christianity, and now defended it on novel grounds, or at least with a different emphasis from that of most contemporary apologists. He regarded the traditional arguments from miracles and fulfilment of prophecy as less important than what he called the 'internal marks of divinity' in the Christian religion. He argued that the system of religion and morality found in the New Testament was so much superior to anything previously known that it must be of divine origin. He particularly stressed the new values inculcated by Christianity, the rejection of active courage, patriotism, and friendship in favour of meekness, forgiveness, and charity towards all men. His emphasis on the uniqueness of Christian moral teaching might seem incompatible with Paley's view that this teaching only enforced by new sanctions what was already discoverable by reason. Paley, however, was impressed by Jenyns's book and made use of it in the chapter of his *Evidences* where he discussed the morality of the gospel.[50]

Here he began by restating the view that the purpose of revelation was to supply sanctions not precepts. In a civilized society men can generally judge tolerably well how they ought to act, but without the assurance of a future state they lack sufficient motive to make them do their duty. This motive was supplied by the Christian revelation.

'And although in doing this, by the ministry of the same person by which this is done, moral precepts, or examples, or illustrations of moral precepts, may be occasionally given, and be highly valuable, yet they do not form the original purpose of the mission.' He goes on to argue that there can be no discoveries in morals similar to those in natural science; 'the qualities of actions depend entirely upon their effects, which effects have been the subject of human experience'. We establish rules based on their tendency to promote human happiness, and refer our actions to these rules and 'in the formation of these rules there is no place for discovery properly so called, but there is ample room for the exercise of wisdom, judgement and prudence'. Christ's teaching is commended not as superior to but as identical with that of the best philosophers. The summary of the law which he gave to the lawyer's inquiry expresses, Paley asserts, precisely what 'the most applauded philosopher of the most enlightened age of the world' might have said if asked for a general rule of life.

This seems hardly compatible with Jenyns's insistence on the new values which Christ's teaching involved. Paley claims to be in complete agreement with Jenyns; he acknowledges the originality of the command not to resist evil, and allows that 'the preference of the patient to the heroic character' is peculiar to Christianity. Yet his agreement does not seem to go very deep. He remarks that the heroic character, the quality which produces the great general or great statesman, may occasionally be beneficial, and he maintains that Christian precepts such as that which advocates turning the other cheek relate to personal conduct from personal motives and do not apply to what is done for the general welfare.

Another characteristic of the gospel morality to which Paley draws attention is the importance attached to the regulation of the thoughts. 'Whosoever looketh on a woman to lust after her hath committed adultery with her already in his heart.' Paley had quoted this saying in his *Moral Philosophy*,[51] but only at the end of an argument designed to show that irregular sexual relations were wrong because their ultimate effect was harmful to an institution productive of human happiness, that of marriage. A strictly utilitarian morality would consider only the effect of actions, and although thoughts may well lead to action they do not necessarily do so. Paley's statement that the qualities of actions depend entirely on their effects seems to exclude from consideration the motive of action or the state of mind from which the action might originate. This is hardly the teaching of the gospels.

'Christ came into the world to tell us that we should go to hell if our actions did not tend to promote the greatest happiness of the greatest number.' This is Leslie Stephen's summary of Paley's position,[52] and it is not wholly unfair. There are passages in his sermons, however, where he speaks with a rather different voice, and says, or implies, that thoughts are as important as actions and that the true motive for action should be not hope of future reward or fear of punishment but the love of God.[53] Such passages might be thought to have more of the spirit of Christianity than Paley's ingenious attempts to equate the morality of the gospel with utilitarianism.

* 6 *
Political Philosophy

As the title of his book shows, Paley regarded political philosophy as closely allied to moral philosophy. He pointed out that the part a man plays in political affairs is as much a question of personal duty as is the conduct of his private life. Moreover, his system of morality was based on the necessity of general rules; having established this principle it was natural and easy for him to proceed to political questions, where the principle is particularly applicable.[1] In his Cambridge lecture notes there are sections on the origin of civil government and the reasons for the subject's submission to government, on taxation and on trade and commerce;[2] but most of the material in this part of his published work appears to have been new. It was, we may surmise, inspired less by his experiences as a college tutor than by his discussions in the Hyson club and his defence of the *status quo* against reformers such as Jebb.

After tracing the origins of government from the family and the tribe Paley poses the question how submission to civil government is maintained, and as in the case of property so in that of government he puts the problem in a provocative manner:

Could we view our own species from a distance, or regard mankind with the same sort of observation with which we read the natural history, or remark the *manners*, of any other animals, there is nothing in the human character which would more surprise us, than the almost universal subjugation of strength to weakness—than to see many millions of robust men, in the complete use and exercise of their personal faculties, and without any defect of courage, waiting upon the will of a child, a woman, a driveller, or a lunatic. And although, when we suppose a vast empire in absolute subjection to one person, and that one depressed beneath the level of his species by infirmities, or vice, we suppose perhaps an extreme case; yet in all cases, even in the most popular forms of government, *the physical strength resides in the governed.*[3]

The answer to the problem is that some obey from prejudice (opinion, that is, not founded on argument), which in the case of hereditary monarchies is reinforced by religious sentiment, others from reason, and others again as a result of self-interest. The wise ruler will bear in mind that physical strength lies with the governed, and will therefore see that his subjects are respected. Civil authority is founded on opinion and opinion should 'be treated with deference and managed with delicacy and circumspection'. Every innovation diminishes the stability of government, and 'some absurdities are to be retained, and many small inconveniences endured in every country, rather than that the usage should be violated, or the course of public affairs diverted from their old and smooth channel. Since one of the chief preservatives of authority is the inability of subjects to unite, the state should both guard against actual combinations and prevent the collecting together of men united by some particular interest or emotion.'[4]

Having explained the causes of obedience Paley turns to the duty of obedience. He rejects the theory, particularly associated with Locke, of a social compact, or contract. Such a compact is a fiction, and if it never in fact took place it has no validity. Moreover, the theory is harmful in its effects on society. If the principles of private contracts are to apply, the subject must be bound by his bargain and must accept the established government however absurd and inconvenient it is. 'No form of government contains a provision for its dissolution', and under the contract theory despotic governments cannot be changed or mitigated. The analogy of the private contract could also lead to the conclusion that every violation of the compact on the part of the ruler releases the subject from his allegiance, and as the terms of the compact are nowhere defined it would be easy for the seditious to claim its violation as a pretext for withdrawing their obedience.[5]

To those who have followed Paley's earlier argument it will come as no surprise to find that after thus rejecting the theory of a social compact he claims that the only ground of the subject's obligation is 'the will of God, as collected from expediency'. God wills the happiness of mankind; civil society conduces to that end; society cannot be upheld unless the interest of the whole is binding on every member. So long therefore as the interest of the whole society requires it, that is, so long as the established government cannot be resisted or changed without public inconvenience, it is the will of God that the established government be obeyed. To which Paley adds the important qualification 'and no longer'. This being so, the justice of a particular case of resistance is no more than a computation of the quantity of grievance on the one side and the probability and cost of redressing it on the other. And each man must judge this for himself. It follows that it may be as much a duty at one time to resist a government as at another to obey it. Encroachment on the subject's rights or abuse of power by the chief magistrate does not justify resistance unless its consequences are sufficiently great to outweigh the evils of civil disturbance. But 'no usage, law, or authority whatever, is so binding, that it need or ought to be continued, when it may be changed with advantage to the community'. The various elements in the constitution are not fixed and immutable principles; they can be changed like other laws when expediency requires it.[6]

Finally, the general happiness of a society is not to be sacrificed to the convenience of a part. This principle Paley tries to apply to an act of resistance, or rebellion, which was fresh in the minds of himself and his readers, that which established American independence. If he had been an American, he claims, he would have had to satisfy himself not only that secession would be beneficial to America but also that this benefit would compensate what Britain would lose. The criterion is the number of individuals who would benefit. If a dependency is small and sparsely populated its interests should be sacrificed to those of the mother country, but when its members increase so as to bear a considerable proportion to the total interest of the community, it may well be that subjection impairs the general happiness as well as its own.[7]

Having argued the question of civil rights and obligations by the light of nature, Paley turns to Revelation. He finds no passage in the New Testament which affects the conclusions he has already arrived at. The Scriptures inculcate the duty of submission, but do not specify the extent of it. Properly interpreted they give no support to unlimited passive obedience or to superstitious ideas of the regal character. 'The divine right of *Kings* is, like the divine right of constables—the law of the land, or even actual and quiet possession of their office; a right ratified, we humbly presume, by the divine approbation, so long as obedience to their authority appears to be necessary, or conducive to the common welfare. Princes are ordained by God by virtue only of that general decree, by which he assents, and adds the sanction of his will, to every law of society, which promotes his own purpose, the communication of human happiness.'[8] The doctrine of the divine right of kings, at least in its old form, must have been pretty well dead by the time that Paley wrote; none the less he thought it advisable in later editions to alter 'constables' to 'other magistrates'.

In a chapter on different forms of government[9] Paley makes use of the old threefold division into monarchy, aristocracy, and democracy, and includes traditional material in discussing their advantages and disadvantages. He adds, however, some characteristic arguments in favour of a democratic, or partly democratic, constitution. One is that it has a salutary effect on the upper classes, who are encouraged to cultivate those faculties which qualify men for deliberation and debate instead of falling into 'sottish habits of animal gratification'or devoting themselves to 'those futile arts and decorations which compose the business and recommendations of a court'. A further advantage is that elections ensure courteous treatment of the common people; 'that contemptuous and overbearing insolence, with which the lower orders of the community are wont to be treated by the higher, is greatly mitigated where the people having something to give'. Finally there is the pleasure which the citizens of a free country derive from knowing what is going on in the world of politics, a subject which provides 'a moderate engagement of the thoughts, without rising to any painful degree of anxiety—or ever leaving a fixed oppression upon the spirits—and what is this, but the end and aim of all those amusements, which compose so much of the business of life and of the value of riches?'

One might have expected that a man like Paley, who believed that nothing was immutable and anything could be changed whenever expediency required, would have found a good deal in contemporary institutions that could well be changed. In fact when he comes to discuss the British Constitution he is a thorough conservative. He does not regard it as perfect and sacrosanct, but he finds it as least as good as can be expected, and certainly not bad enough to justify any change. His defence of it is based on two main considerations. One is that political changes often produce effects other than those intended. 'The direct consequence is often the least important. Incidental, remote, and unthought-of evil or advantages frequently exceed the good that is designed, or the mischief that is foreseen. It is from the silent and unobserved operation, from the obscure progress of causes set to work for different purposes, that the greatest revolutions take their rise.'[10] The second consideration is that institutions apparently quite anomalous can be made to work and do in fact work much better than might be supposed. Thus the House of Lords might seem ill constituted to be the highest court of appeal, formed as it is of men born to their station or ennobled for reasons quite unconnected with legal knowledge. In fact the practice of placing in the House of Lords some of the most eminent judges means that the rest of the body inevitably defers to the opinions of the experts.[11]

'There is one end of civil government peculiar to a good constitution, namely the happiness of its subjects; there is another end essential to a good government, but common to it with many bad ones—its own preservation.'[12] The British constitution provides for both. Every citizen is capable of being a member of Parliament, and every member may propose whatever law he pleases. Everyone has his representative to whom he can forward his complaints, and the representatives are so intermixed with the constituents and the constituents with the rest of the people that they cannot impose any burden in which they do not themselves share, while they are so far dependent on their constituents that the best way of commending themselves is to devise or support beneficial laws. The institution of monarchy serves to preserve tranquillity, and the possible dangers of regal government are avoided by the fact that taxation is kept in the hands of the Commons and the citizen is protected against arbitrary punishment. The constitution provides for its own preservation by the system of checks and balances which ensures that no one element, King, Lords, or Commons, can encroach on another and that if they attempt to do so the other two will unite to resist.[13]

The House of Lords has the advantage of enabling the King to reward the servants of the public at small expense to the nation; it helps to secure the stability of regal government and it 'stems the progress of popular fury'. Popular fury was not perhaps much in evidence in the eighteenth-century House of Commons, but, as Paley says, occasions could arise when the commonwealth might be saved by the reluctance of the nobility to yield to the common people. 'We do not suppose the nobility to be more unprejudiced than others; we only suppose that their prejudices are different from those of others.'[14]

As for the House of Commons, Paley candidly admits those anomalies in parliamentary representation which are well known to the modern student of British history. As he puts it, 'about half of the House of Commons obtain their seats in that assembly by the election of the people, the other half by purchase, or by the nomination of single proprietors of great estates'. There is a 'flagrant incongruity' here, but one which reflection shows to be far less objectionable than it appears at first sight. Representation is not a natural right; it is a right only so far as it conduces to public utility. 'If men the most likely by their qualifications to know and promote the public interest be actually returned to Parliament, it signifies little who return them.' The existing House of Commons includes the leading landowners and merchants, the heads of the army, the navy and the law, the occupiers of great offices in the state and many eminent private individuals. Would any new scheme bring together more wisdom and integrity?[15]

Even those features which seem most objectionable can be defended. The existing system ensures that many seats can only be held by men of large fortunes, and this means that the most weighty and influential members of the community are enlisted in support of the claims of the Commons. The very variety of tenures and qualifications on which voting rites are based has the advantage of introducing into Parliament a variety of characters and professions. The most able members are commonly found among the representatives of small boroughs; when these are for sale the men most likely to become purchasers are those with sufficient talents to make the best of their bargain. If some seats are in the hands of the nobility this serves to maintain an alliance between the two Houses and to associate a powerful part of the nation with the Commons.

Paley then turns to the influence of the Crown, the diminution of which was the main object of schemes of reform. After observing that a better way of proceeding would be to make a direct reduction of Crown patronage he raises the question whether it is really desirable to lessen this patronage. He puts the case for it as contributing to cohesion and stability, as an element which can counteract the 'restless arrogating spirit' of popular assemblies. He makes it clear that he is not condoning bribery; what he does accept is the influence which results from the acceptance or expectation of public preferment, which, he maintains, does not involve a sacrifice of personal probity. 'If you remove the influence of the Crown, it is only to make way for influence from a different quarter. If motives of expectation and gratitude be withdrawn, other motives will succeed in their place, acting probably in an opposite direction, but equally irrelative and external to the proper merits of the question.'[16]

Such is Paley's defence of 'bribery and corruption'. It is successful up to a point, but it goes too far. It may be true that some of the ablest members of Parliament sat for small boroughs (Pitt is an outstanding example), but it is hard to believe that the quality of the Commons was improved by the purchase of seats. Paley himself gives the impression of being a little uncomfortable about his defence of the influence of the Crown. He deserts his usual habit of clear and definite statement and hides behind the opinion of 'many wise and virtuous politicians' and those 'who consider stability amongst the first perfections of any government'. A small detail shows that he realized he had gone a little too far. In his first edition he wrote: 'but whilst we dispute concerning different schemes of reformation all directed to the same end, a previous doubt occurs in the debate, whether the end itself be good, *or even innocent*—whether the influence so loudly complained of can be destroyed, or *even diminished, with safety* to the state'. In the second edition the sentence became: '. . . whether the end itself be good, *or safe*—whether the influence so loudly complained of can be destroyed, or *even much diminished, without danger* to the state'.[17] Paley shows that the existing Constitution worked tolerably well in spite of its anomalies; he does not show that there was any real danger in reform. If he had lived until 1832, his realism would probably have prevented him from the error of which he convicted his country in connection with the loss of the American colonies, that of 'not perceiving the point of time when the irresistible order and progress of human affairs demanded a change of laws and policy'.[18]

From the legislature Paley turns to the administration of justice and the theory of crime and punishment. Here again his discussion is in effect a defence of the British system of his day. This system combined a criminal code of great severity with an extremely liberal criminal procedure.[19] The criminal law imposed the death penalty on an excessively large number of crimes, about two hundred in all, some of them by modern standards quite minor offences. On the other hand it could justly be claimed that the administration of the law was fair and impartial and thoroughly safeguarded the rights of the accused.

In a weighty chapter on the administration of justice Paley discusses the principles of jurisprudence and finds the English system of administration satisfactory in all respects but two. The first is the rule that juries must be unanimous, the second is the constitution of the House of Lords as the final court of appeal. Both, however, work better than might be expected, the latter for reasons given above, the former because in criminal prosecutions the rule operates in favour of the prisoner while in civil suits it adds weight to the directions of the judge. Apart from these minor defects Paley has nothing but praise for the English system.

A politician who should sit down to delineate a plan for the dispensation of public justice, guarded against all access to influence and corruption, and bringing together the separate advantages of knowledge and impartiality, would find, when he had done, that he had been transcribing the judicial constitution of England. And it may teach the most discontented amongst us to acquiesce in the government of his country, to reflect, that the pure, and wise, and equal administration of the laws, forms the first end and blessing of social union; and that this blessing is enjoyed by him in a perfection, which he will seek in vain in another nation of the world.[20]

This picture might be thought a little too complacent, but it is confirmed by the admiration which foreign visitors expressed for the English system.[21] To quote only one, F. de la Rochefoucaud, who visited the country only a year before the publication of Paley's work, wrote: 'The administration of justice in England deserves the highest commendation. On two occasions I was myself a witness of the equitable way in which English criminal, as well as civil, cases are conducted, and I can testify that almost against my will I was filled with respect and admiration.'[22]

Foreign observers did not accord the same admiration to the criminal code, which Paley defended in what Sir Leon Radzinowicz describes as a 'masterly exposition'.[23] 'The proper end of human punishment is not the satisfaction of justice, but the prevention of crimes.'[24] Justice requires that punishment should be in proportion to guilt. Only God, from whom nothing is hidden, can judge of the guilt and apportion the punishment accordingly. Men with their imperfect knowledge must proceed otherwise. The only consideration which authorizes punishment by human laws is the danger to society which would result from absence of punishment. Thus crimes are punished in proportion to the difficulty and the necessity of preventing them; stealing from a shop may not be worse morally than stealing from a private house, but is rightly punished more severely. Sheep stealing, horse stealing, and the stealing of cloth from tenters or bleaching grounds are capital offences, not because the crimes are in their nature more heinous than some which receive a lesser punishment, but 'because the property being more exposed requires the terror of a capital punishment to protect it'.[25]

There are two methods, Paley points out, of administering penal justice. One assigns capital punishments to few offences and inflicts it invariably, the other assigns it to many but inflicts it in only a few examples of each kind. The latter was in use in England, where of those who received sentence of death scarcely one in ten, according to Paley, was executed.[26] This system meets with his approval.

By the number of statutes creating capital offences, it sweeps into the net every crime, which under any possible circumstances, may merit the punishment of death; but when the execution of this sentence comes to be deliberated upon, a small proportion of each class are singled out, the general character or the peculiar aggravations of whose crimes render them fit examples of public justice. By this expedient few actually suffer death, whilst the dread and danger of it hang over the crimes of many. . . . The wisdom and humanity of this design furnish a just excuse for the multiplicity of capital offences, which the laws of England are accused of creating beyond those of other countries. The charge of cruelty is answered by observing that these laws were never meant to be carried into indiscriminate execution; that the legislature, when it establishes its last and highest sanctions, trusts to the benignity of the Crown to relax their severity, as often as circumstances appear to palliate the offence, or even as often as those circumstances of aggravation are wanting, which rendered this rigorous interposition necessary.[27]

If in England far more crimes were punished by death than elsewhere, this was justified by the degree of liberty allowed, by the existence of great cities, and by the absence of any punishment short of death sufficiently severe to act as a deterrent. This last consideration leads Paley to a new point. The end of punishment is not only the prevention of crimes; it is also the reformation of criminals. He sees little chance of reformation resulting from existing punishments, but has some hopes that solitary confinement, which was not a punishment in use at the time, would have a reformatory as well as a deterrent effect. There remained the difficulty of disposing of criminals after their term of imprisonment. On this point Paley has a positive suggestion to make, that discharged prisoners should be distributed in the country, detained within certain limits, and employed on the roads, while female prisoners might be put in charge of the overseers of country parishes, housed, and provided with the materials of occupation.[28]

Paley recognizes that 'a vigilant magistracy, an accurate police, a proper distribution of force and intelligence, together with due rewards for the discovery and apprehension of malefactors ... contribute more to the suppression of crime than any violent exacerbations of punishment'. But like most of his fellow countrymen he would have been reluctant to see any infringement of the traditional liberties of Englishmen. He gives what Sir Leon Radzinowicz calls 'a brilliant summary of what a Continental police really was',[29] and claims that such a system, though efficient, was only possible under arbitrary governments.

Neither the spirit of the laws, nor of the people, will suffer the detention or confinement of suspected persons, without proof of their guilt, which it is often impossible to obtain; nor will they allow that masters of families be obliged to record and render up a description of the strangers or inmates whom they entertain; nor that an account be demanded, at the pleasure of the magistrate, of each man's time, employment, and means of subsistence; nor securities to be required when these accounts appear unsatisfactory or dubious; nor men to be apprehended upon the mere suggestion of idleness or vagrancy; nor to be confined to certain districts; nor the inhabitants of each district to be made responsible for one another's behaviour; nor passports to be exacted from all persons entering or leaving the kingdom; least of all will they tolerate the appearance of an armed force, or of military law; or suffer the streets and public roads to be guarded and patrolled by soldiers; or lastly, entrust the police with such discretionary powers, as may make sure of the guilty, however they involve the innocent.[30]

It may seem strange that so kindly and humane a man as Paley should have defended what today seems a savage and barbarous criminal code. His defence, however, is in line with his theory that acts must be judged by their general consequences. The individual must be sacrificed to the interests of the community as a whole, and one must consider the remoter as well as the immediate consequences. The extent to which Paley carries his theory can be seen from the alarmist picture he paints of the consequences which would ensue if the death penalty did not check the crimes of forgery, counterfeiting the coinage, and stealing letters in the course of conveyance. Trade would decline and depopulation would follow, 'till solitude and barrenness over-spread the land; until a desolation similar to what obtains in many countries of Asia, which were once the most civilised and frequented parts of the world, succeed in the place of crowded cities, of cultivated fields, of happy and well populated regions'. Though the immediate consequence of these crimes may be only to deprive an individual of a small part of his property, their ultimate effect is 'the laying waste of human existence'.[31]

Paley's doctrine is open to criticism not only on grounds of penal theory and humanitarianism but also on practical grounds. The criminal law did not have the intended deterrent effect. The eighteenth century multiplied capital offences, but crime did not decrease. None the less Paley's views were accepted by the leading members of the legal profession of his day. When Sir S. Romilly brought forward his proposals for legal reform in 1810 the Lord Chancellor and the Lord Chief Justice supported Paley's doctrine of punishment; the Lord Chief Justice, Paley's old friend Lord Ellenborough, in his speeches in the Lords did little more than summarize his views, while Romilly found it necessary to speak at length in refutation of them.[32] Even in 1836, when the main reforms had been effected, the Commissioners responsible for the Second Report on Criminal Law prefaced their recommendations with a critical examination of Paley's views, which they said were 'all that could be said for the practice by an eminently acute and skilful reasoner', and were 'the arguments chiefly relied upon by those who have defended it when subjected to Parliamentary discussion'.[33]

It should not, however, be supposed that Paley did no more than defend the existing system. He had some suggestions to make for reform. He was in favour of exempting from the death penalty the offence of privately stealing from the person (picking pockets), and advocated distinguishing between different kinds of forgery, which as the law then was were punished 'with undistinguishing severity'.[34] He was opposed to public executions on the ground that they were demoralizing to the onlooker, or if they aroused pity for the criminal failed to have the required exemplary effect. He held that 'infamous punishments' (the pillory and the stocks) were mismanaged, and would be better employed in the punishment of some 'offences of higher life'.[35] While defending the imprisonment of insolvent debtors as a punishment, he recognized that punishment was not justified without a crime and hoped for an alteration in the law which would distinguish degrees of guilt.[36] Finally, he lays it down that 'a law being found to produce no sensible good effects is a sufficient reason for repealing it, as adverse and injurious to the rights of a free citizen, without demanding specific evidence of its bad effects'. This maxim, he goes on to say, 'might be remembered in a revision of many laws of this country; especially of the game laws; of the poor laws, so far as they lay restrictions upon the poor themselves; of the laws against Papists and Dissenters: and, amongst people enamoured to excess and jealous of their liberty, it seems a matter of surprise that this principle has been so imperfectly attended to'.[37]

In connection with his discussion of religious establishments, to which we shall return in a later chapter, Paley argued for a combination of a national religion with complete toleration for those who dissented from it, except perhaps where religious views were united with political attitudes hostile to the country's constitution. In making this qualification he had in mind the connection between Popery and Jacobitism. But he points out that this connection was accidental in its origin and would probably be only temporary in its duration; the restrictions on Roman Catholics ought therefore to last no longer than they were necessary for the preservation of public tranquillity. Otherwise, and apart from the case of the Quakers, whose refusal to bear arms made it absurd for them to hold military command, he saw no reason why men of different religious views should not 'sit on the same bench, deliberate in the same council, or fight in the same ranks, as well as men of various and opposite opinions upon a controverted topic of natural philosophy, history, or ethics'.[38] There was also, he believed, a positive merit in toleration; it led to the investigation and discovery of truth. He held the optimistic view that if different religions were professed without restriction in the same country, the best, or, as he put it, the most rational religion would prevail. 'I do not mean that men will formally renounce their ancient religion, but that they will adopt into it the more rational doctrines, the improvements and discoveries of the neighbouring sect; by which the worse religion, without the ceremony of a reformation, will insensibly assimilate itself to the better. If Popery, for instance, and Protestantism were permitted to dwell quietly together, Papists might not become Protestants (for the name is commonly the last thing that is changed), but they would become more enlightened and informed; they would by little and little incorporate into their creed many of the tenets of Protestantism as well as imbibe a portion of its spirit and moderation.'[39] This forecast was hardly fulfilled, at any rate in the short run. English Catholicism after Emancipation did not imbibe the spirit of Paley's moderate and enlightened Protestantism; rather it reacted against that spirit and firmly asserted its exclusive claims.

Paley's Cambridge lectures included material on trade and commerce and on taxation, but in his published work the chapter on what we today would call economics is headed 'Of Population and Provision, and of Agriculture and Commerce as subservient thereto'. It is based on a principle which he later modified, the rather naive principle that the greater the population the greater the sum of human happiness. If one compares adjoining periods in the same country, he maintains, the collective happiness will be nearly in the exact proportion of the numbers; in other circumstances it may not be quite so great, but any considerable increase of numbers will usually involve an increase of happiness. The decay of population is the greatest evil a state can suffer, and its increase should be the aim of all statesmen in preference to false ideas of national grandeur. 'The final view of all rational politics is to produce the greatest quantity of happiness in a given tract of country. The riches, strength, and glory of nations; the topics which history celebrates, and which alone almost engage the praises, and possess the admiration of mankind, have no value further than as they contribute to this end.' And 'although we speak of communities as of sentient beings; although we ascribe to them happiness and misery, desires, interests, and passions, nothing really exists or feels but *individuals*. The happiness of a people is made up of the happiness of single persons.'[40]

In order to encourage population one of the first needs is a flourishing agriculture, and to ensure this the full advantage of any improvement should go to the improver and no one should share in the profit who does not assist in the production. For this reason, as we have already seen, Paley, in this respect like Adam Smith, condemned the institution of tithes. Trade, he held, is useful so far as its contributes to population; it keeps employed those who do not work on the land, and it stimulates the industry of those who do by providing articles which they are tempted to want. Provided that it employs sufficient numbers, it does not matter how unnecessary are the articles which it supplies. Taxation is not necessarily harmful to population and can be beneficial if rightly directed.

Paley's views on taxation, though based on his theory of population, are of interest even apart from that theory. A modern writer has praised him for a grasp of distributional concepts far excelling that of his contemporaries and claimed that in emphasizing the effects of tax distribution on the country's general welfare he virtually anticipated modern theory.[41] Taxes, Paley observes, do not diminish the public stock; they only vary the distribution of it. They can be harmful if they result in money passing from the industrious to the idle, from the many to the few, and if their produce 'is expended upon a train of gentry, in the maintaining of pomp, or in the purchase of influence'. The wise statesman, however, will adjust his taxes so as to give 'the least possible obstruction to those means of subsistence by which the mass of the community is maintained'.[42] To this end Paley makes two proposals. One is that there should be abatements or exemptions to married persons and parents with a certain number of children. The other is that taxation should be progressive, or graduated; the important consideration is not what men have but what they can spare, and a man with £1000 can more easily give up £100 than one with £100 can give up £10. Similar proposals for graduated taxation were put forward by Tom Paine, and this, Paley maintained in conversation, was why they were not adopted when Pitt introduced income tax in 1799. 'Tom was the black dog and his name was sufficient reason for rejecting the measure; nothing could be good that came from Tom.'[43] Pitt included allowances for dependent children, though these were abandoned in 1806 and not reintroduced until Lloyd George's budget of 1909. The same budget introduced the principle of graduation in the imposition of what was then called supertax, and this was itself made subject to graduation in 1914.[44]

'On the subject of population I cannot agree with Archdeacon Paley, who says that the quantity of happiness in any country is best measured by the number of people.' So wrote Malthus in an unpublished pamphlet of 1796.[45] Two years later he wrote his famous *Essay on Population*, in which he argued that population naturally increases faster than the means of subsistence. Paley was convinced, and Malthus used to say that he and Pitt were the two converts of whom he was most proud.[46] In the course of his last work, *Natural Theology*, Paley found occasion to introduce a summary of Malthus's views, but it cannot be said that he subjected his earlier opinions to a thorough revision. His natural cheerfulness could not be damped by the depressing prospect opened up by Malthus. He remained optimistic.

> It need not, however, dishearten any endeavours for the public service, to know that population naturally treads upon the heels of improvement. If the condition of a people be meliorated, the consequence will be either that the *mean* happiness will be increased, or a greater number partake of it; or, which is most likely to happen, that both effects will take place together. There may be limits fixed by nature to both, but they are limits not yet attained, nor even approached, in any country of the world.[47]

This passage comes from his chapter on the goodness of the deity. His last thoughts on human society are part of his theodicy. They show him disposed as ever to see the best in things as they are, and to argue that the supposed ills of life in this world are less than they appear to be. Advantages of wealth and station, he maintains, are small in comparison with those provided by nature. Ambition has its pleasures, but authority is not necessarily pleasant; 'command is anxiety, obedience ease'. Artificial distinctions such as those conferred

by birth, position, or the esteem attached to certain professions have
the advantage of counteracting the inevitable differences of wealth.
Wealth certainly brings advantages, but these are not greater than they
should be.

Money is the sweetener of human toil; the substitute for coercion;
the reconciler of labour with liberty. It is, moreover, the stimulant of
enterprise in all projects and undertakings, as well as of diligence
in the most beneficial arts and employments. Now did affluence,
when possessed, contribute nothing to happiness, or nothing beyond
the mere supply of necessaries; and the secret should come to be
discovered; we might be in danger of losing great part of the uses,
which are, at present, derived to us through this important medium.
Not only would the tranquillity of social life be put in peril by the
want of a motive to attach men to their private concerns; but the
satisfaction which all men receive from success in their respective
occupations, which collectively constitutes the great mass of human
comfort, would be done away in its very principle.[48]

❖ 7 ❖
Natural Theology

Natural Theology is theology as it can be deduced from the world of nature. In the Christian era it has commonly been contrasted with the theology of revealed religion, but the term was used and the main arguments developed before the Christian revelation. Its main aspect, and that with which we are here concerned, is the 'argument from design', the belief that the nature and existence of God can be deduced from the evidence of design in the world. Kant, who regarded the argument as insufficient in itself to prove God's existence, none the less called it 'the oldest, the clearest and that most in conformity with the common reason of humanity'.[1]

This argument is found in all its essentials in the brief conversation between Socrates and a certain Aristodemus reported by Xenophon, in which Socrates observes that man has been provided with eyes, ears, and other organs perfectly adapted for their purpose, and argues that these cannot be the result of chance but must be the contrivance of a wise and beneficent creator.[2] It was particularly developed by the Stoics, and found its classic expression in antiquity in the second book of Cicero's *De Natura Deorum*. 'What can be clearer or more obvious,' asks the Stoic spokesman in the dialogue, 'when we look up to heaven and observe the celestial bodies, than that there is a power possessed of surpassing mind by which it is guided?'[3] A universe so constituted that it could not be better in respect of either utility or beauty cannot be fortuitous; there must be some being which not only guides and directs it but is as it were its architect.[4] Analogies are drawn from the artefacts of man, a house, a statue, a ship, a sundial or water clock, and in particular from the planetarium recently constructed by Posidonius, which would convince anyone even in the barbarous regions of Britain or Scythia that it was the work of reason.[5] The Stoic spokesman then passes on to the vegetable and animal kingdom and finally to man. He dwells on the human eye (the example which was to recur again and again in later developments of the argument) and the other organs of sense, and on man's power of reason and gift of speech. The whole universe, he concludes, was created for the benefit of man.[6]

These arguments passed into Christian theology. They were repeated by Lactantius, with the difference that whereas the Stoics had tended to identify God with the universe, he clearly separated the creator from his creation and argued that if God made the universe he must have an existence independent of it.[7] The Middle Ages preferred *a priori* methods of arguing, and it was not until the growth of modern science in the seventeenth century that the argument from design came to the fore again. The discoveries of Newton, popularized by the young Bentley in his Boyle lectures, showed the universe as the work of a mind which had devised the heavenly bodies on mathematical principles. To quote Addison's hymn,

> The spacious firmament on high,
> With all the blue ethereal sky,
> And spangled heavens, a shining frame,
> Their great Original proclaim.

Study of terrestrial life led to the same conclusion. John Ray the naturalist wrote on *The Wisdom of God manifested in the Works of Creation* (1691). William Derham wrote not only *Astro-Theology: a Demonstration of the Being and Attributes of God from a Survey of the Heavens* but also *Physico-Theology: a Demonstration of the Being and Attributes of God from his Works of Creation* (1715; 1713). Plants, animals, and human beings joined with the celestial bodies in proclaiming 'The hand that made us is divine'. A typical utterance of the mid-eighteenth century is that of Colin Maclaurin:

The plain argument for the existence of the Deity, obvious to all and carrying irresistible conviction with it, is from the evident contrivance and fitness of things for one another which we find in the universe. There is no need of nice or subtle reasonings in the matter; a manifest contrivance suggests a contriver. It strikes us like a sensation; and artful reasonings against it may puzzle us but it is without shaking our belief. No person, for example, that knows the principles of optics and the structure of the eye can believe that it was formed without skill in that science; or that male and female in animals were not formed for each other and for continuing the species.[8]

A sceptical criticism of the argument was advanced by Hume in his posthumous *Dialogues concerning Natural Religion*. The analogy, says Philo, the spokesman of scepticism, who is presumed to represent Hume's own views, between the contrivances of man and those of the Creator is imperfect; a house presupposes an architect, but the universe is not sufficiently similar to a house to justify the assumption of a similar cause. Design is only one of the principles of the universe. 'What peculiar privilege has this little agitation of the brain which we call thought, that we must thus make it the model of the whole universe?'[9] There is much that is inexplicable in the works of nature and no proof can be drawn from them that the Deity is perfect or is a unity. The most that can be said is that the cause or causes of order in the universe probably bear some remote analogy to human intelligence.[10] Hume's scepticism, however, had done little to shake the widely accepted view when Paley restated it vigorously, confidently, with no great subtlety but with an impressive grasp of his material, in his *Natural Theology*.

He begins with his famous analogy of the watch. There was nothing new about this; similar analogies had been used, as we have seen, as long ago as Cicero.[11] Paley with his flair for catching the attention of the reader, adopts it to make an effective opening to his argument.

> In crossing a heath, suppose I pitched my foot against a *stone*, and were asked how the stone came to be there; I might possibly answer, that, for any thing I knew to the contrary, it had lain there for ever .... But suppose I had found a *watch* upon the ground, and it should be enquired how the watch happened to be in that place; I should hardly think of the answer which I had before given, that for any thing I knew, the watch might have always been there. Yet why should not this answer serve for the watch as well as for the stone? ... For this reason, and for no other, viz. that, when we come to inspect the watch, we perceive (what we could not discover in the stone) that its several parts are framed and put together for a purpose.

He goes on, with that interest in contrivances of all kinds that had been his throughout life, to describe in detail the workings of the watch, and concludes that these would clearly show it to have had a maker. Next he imagines the finder of the watch discovering that it had the property of producing another watch like itself. This would not affect the argument. The watch that produced another watch could not be said to have constructed it; the designing mind must always be assumed, however far back we go, and the discovery that the watch reproduces itself can only increase our admiration for the skill used in its formation. Here the reader may hesitate to follow Paley, for watches do not in fact produce watches. Hume had observed that the world resembled an animal or vegetable rather than a watch;[12] Paley tries to make a watch resemble an animal.

Paley does not make much of 'the spacious firmament on high'. Much of the material in his chapter on astronomy was obtained for him by John Law from the professor of astronomy at Dublin. He was sceptical of its value for the purpose of his argument. 'My opinion of astronomy has always been that it is *not* the best medium through which to prove the agency of an intelligent Creator, but that this being proved, it shows beyond all other sciences, the magnificence of his operations.' Our ignorance of the heavenly bodies is too great for us to apply any analogy; we have nothing with which to compare them. What is wonderful is that we understand as much of astronomy as we do.[13]

Evidently Paley had little interest in astronomy. He was, however, a keen student of natural history, and had collected much information from reading and observation to illustrate design in the works of nature. Inevitably he makes much of the human eye, the examination of which, according to one of his predecessors, was a cure for atheism.[14]

Were there no example in the world of contrivance except that of the *eye*, it would be alone sufficient to support the conclusion which we draw from it, as to the necessity of an intelligent Creator.... Its coats and humours, constructed, as the lenses of a telescope are constructed, for the refraction of rays of light to a point, which forms the proper action of the organ; the provision in its muscular tendons for turning its pupil to the object, similar to that which is given to the telescope by screws...; the further provision for its defence, for its constant lubricity and moisture, which we see in its socket and its lids, in its gland for the secretion of the matter of tears...; these provisions compose altogether an apparatus, a system of parts, a preparation of means, so manifest in their design, so exquisite in their contrivance, so successful in their issue, so precious and so infinitely beneficial in their use, as, in my opinion, to bear down all doubt that can be raised on the subject.[15]

He proceeds to distinguish the mechanical and the immechanical parts of the body, of which the former, though probably the coarsest parts of nature's workmanship, are those which can most easily be shown as specimens of design. These are the bones and muscles. Paley challenges 'any man to produce, in the joints and pivots of the most complicated or the most flexible machine that was ever contrived, a construction more artificial, or more evidently artificial, than that which is seen in the vertebrae of the human *neck*'.[16] The forearm, the spine, the chest, the knee-pan, and the shoulder-blade show no less evidence of contrivance. Of the joints he particularly dwells on the ball and socket joint, with the ligament, strong and flexible, keeping the two parts firmly in their place. 'If I had been permitted to frame proof of contrivance, such as might satisfy the most distrustful enquirer, I know not whether I could have chosen an example of mechanism more unequivocal, or more free from objection, than this ligament.'[17] From the muscles he passes on to the vessels of animal bodies, the circulation of the blood, and the heart, 'this wonderful machine', which goes 'night and day, for eighty years together, at the rate of a hundred thousand strokes every twenty-four hours, having, at every stroke, a great resistance to overcome', and continues without disorder and without weariness.[18] Another 'exquisite structure' is found in the two pipes going down to the throat, one the passage for the food, the other for the breath and voice. These two functions are performed with almost complete success.

Reflect how frequently we swallow, how constantly we breathe. In a city-feast, for example, what deglutition, what anhelation! yet does this little cartilage, the epiglottis, so effectually interpose its office, so securely guard the entrance of the wind-pipe, that whilst morsel after morsel, draught after draught, are coursing one another over it, an accident of a crumb or a drop slipping into this passage (which nevertheless must be opened for the breath every second of time) excites in the whole company, not only alarm by its danger, but surprise by its novelty. Not two guests are choked in a century.[19]

Our admiration is excited no less by 'the animal structure regarded as a mass'. Everything is in its place and one side exactly corresponds with another. 'It is the most difficult thing that can be to get a wig made even; yet how seldom is the *face* awry!'[20]

Paley surveys the world of nature, birds, fish, insects, and plants, and finds everywhere instances of ingenious contrivance, in the web feet of water fowl, the fang of a viper, the bag of an opossum, the tongue of a woodpecker, the combination in a mole of palmated feet and small sunken eyes, the abdomen of a silkworm ('as incontestably mechanical as a wire drawer's mill'). But it is unnecessary to follow him as he advances instance after instance of the wisdom of the Creator.

A reviewer of Paley's *Natural Theology* observed that unlike previous writers he considered and answered the objections of atheistical writers.[21] The oldest and simplest of such objections was that of Lucretius; *tanta stat praedita culpa*, the world is so faulty.[22] This, however, was primarily an objection to the view that the world was made for the benefit of mankind. This was the view of the Stoics, for whom man, distinguished from the beasts by the possession of reason and akin rather to the gods, was the centre of creation for whose benefit all was designed. Paley does not share this anthropocentric attitude. For him all life has its place in God's design and its share in the happiness he wills.

Here he was probably influenced by Abraham Tucker, who considered it a sign of 'an overweening conceit of man's importance' to 'imagine this stupendous frame of the universe fabricated for him alone' and ventured to offend 'the delicacy of my contemporaries by representing almighty power and wisdom employed in providing conveniences and enjoyments for the pismire, the earthworm, and the mite, the ugly spider, the filthy maggot and the venomous adder'.[23] In the same spirit Paley wrote: 'The hinges in the wings of an earwig, and the joints of its antennae are as highly wrought as if the Creator had had nothing else to finish.'[24] It did not worry him that parts of the earth were uninhabitable by man; they might be filled with happy animals or insects. Some had thought that there was too much water in this world, but 'I know not why the sea may not have as good a right to its place as the land. It may proportionately support as many inhabitants; minister to as large an aggregate of enjoy-ment.'[25]

It is a happy world after all. The air, the earth, the water, teem with delighted existence. In a spring noon, or a summer evening, on whichever side I turn my eyes, myriads of happy beings crowd on my view. 'The insect youth are on the wing.' Swarms of new-born *flies* are trying their pinions in the air. Their sportive motions, their wanton mazes, their gratuitous activity, their continual change of place without use or purpose, testify their joy, and the exultation which they feel in their lately discovered faculties. A *bee* amongst the flowers in spring, is one of the most cheerful objects that can be looked upon. . . . Plants are covered with aphides, greedily sucking their juices, and constantly as it should seem, in the act of sucking. It cannot be doubted but that this is a state of gratification. . . . Other species are *running about*, with an alacrity in their motions, which carries with it every mark of pleasure. . . . If we look to what the *waters* produce, shoals of the fry of fish frequent the margins of rivers, of lakes, and of the sea itself. These are so happy that they know not what to do with themselves. Their attitudes, their vivacity, their leaps out of the water, their frolics in it (which I have noticed a thousand times with equal attention and amusement), all conduce to show their excess of spirits, and are simply the effects of that excess.[26]

'The modern observer', as a recent writer puts it, after quoting part of the above passage, 'sees the swallows and flycatchers preying on this multitude, whose activities, so far from being "gratuitous", are adapted by natural selection for the attraction of mates or the avoidance of enemies.'[27] Paley, though he knew nothing of natural selection, was well aware that animals preyed on one another. He observes, however, that death by violence may be better than death by disease. 'Is it then to see the world filled with drooping, superannuated, half starved helpless animals, that you would alter the present system of pursuit and prey?'[28] Moreover the pursuit of prey seems to constitute the enjoyment of some of the animal creation, while the happiness of the victims does not seem to be diminished by their fears. And the system of destruction among animals can only be considered in relation to the system of fecundity; the prolific generation of so many creatures compensates for predatory activities, while destruction checks excessive generation.

What of man, so prone to suffering and exposed to ills of various kinds? In his case it is not so clear that good predominates over evil. But Paley, repeating some paragraphs from his *Moral and Political Philosophy*, maintains that in creating man God must have intended him to be happy, since evil is never the object of contrivance; teeth were contrived for the purpose of eating, not in order to ache.[29] He acknowledges the existence of evil, and advances various points in explanation of it; but he is perhaps happier with practical considerations than with theoretical arguments. He notes that pain is a salutary provision which gives notice of danger and encourages self-preservation; that its pauses and alleviation give positive pleasure; that few diseases are fatal, and that fatal diseases have the advantage of reconciling us to death; that the fear of death is inseparable from the enjoyment of life. Human life, however, is not a state of unmixed happiness or misery. It is a 'condition calculated for the production, exercise, and improvement, of moral qualities, with a view to a future state'.[30]

Paley has little patience with those who explained the works of nature otherwise than as the work of a designing mind. To invoke 'laws' or 'principles' instead of the agency of personal intelligence was a mere substitution of words for reasons, or a perverse rejection of the obvious explanation simply because it was obvious.

> We know a cause [intelligence] adequate to the appearances, which we wish to account for: we have this cause continually producing similar appearances: yet, rejecting this cause, the sufficiency of which we know, and the action of which is constantly before our eyes, we are invited to resort to suppositions, destitute of a single fact for their support, and confirmed by no analogy with which we are acquainted. Were it necessary to enquire into the *motives* of men's opinions, I mean their motives separate from their arguments; I should almost suspect, that, because the proof of a Deity drawn from the constitution of nature is not only popular but vulgar, (which may arise from the cogency of the proof, and be indeed its highest recommendation,) and because it is a species almost of *puerility* to take up with it; for these reasons, minds, which are habitually in search of invention and originality, feel a restless inclination to strike off into other solutions and other expositions.[31]

Among these perverse innovators was Erasmus Darwin, who took the first tentative steps towards enunciating a theory of evolution in his *Zoonomia*, published in 1794. The theory was that the parts of an animal or plant were not designed for the use to which they are applied but have grown out of that use, that they have by slow improvements acquired the form fitted for their present purpose. The elephant acquired its long proboscis through constant attempts to thrust out its nose; the hump of a camel was the result of carrying heavy burdens; the pouch of a pelican had gradually grown from the habit of storing part of its prey uneaten. This theory, Paley asserts, is contradicted by many phenomena and inadequate to explain others. No such changes have ever been observed. 'All the changes in Ovid's Metamorphoses might have been effected by these appetencies [Erasmus Darwin's word], if the theory were true; yet not an example, nor the pretence of an example is offered of a single change being known to have taken place. . . . The hypothesis remains destitute of evidence.'[32]

It was not Erasmus Darwin but his grandson who undermined the basis of Paley's arguments. If the theory of natural selection is accepted, the existence of a divine artificer cannot be deduced simply from the suitability of human and animal organs for their purpose; without such suitability there would have been no survival. As Darwin wrote, referring to Paley's argument that no organ can be found designed to cause pain or injury to its possessor, 'Natural selection will never produce in a being any structure more injurious than beneficial to that being, for natural selection acts solely by and for the good of each. . . . If any part comes to be injurious it will be modified; or if it be not so, the being will become extinct as myriads have become extinct.'[33]

It would be wholly unhistorical to criticize Paley for not accepting the doctrine of evolution. His arguments were found convincing at the time of writing and were generally accepted during the next fifty years or so. Apart from the collected editions of Paley's works, *Natural Theology* was reprinted many times, including an edition with notes by men of the eminence of Lord Brougham and Sir Charles Bell. Similar works were produced by others. The Earl of Bridgwater, who died in 1829, left money for a series of eight treatises to be published to demonstrate 'the power, wisdom, and goodness of God as manifested in the Creation', to be illustrated by 'the variety and formation of God's creatures in the animal, vegetable and mineral kingdoms; the effect of digestion and thereby of conversion; the construction of the

hand of man, and an infinite variety of other arguments'. The mere
fact that the terms of the will were carried out is hardly in itself
significant; what is significant is that the eight authors whose *Bridgwater Treatises* appeared between 1833 and 1836 included many of
undoubted scientific eminence. Darwin himself had a great admiration
for Paley's work, and found its arguments conclusive until he arrived
at his evolutionary theory.[34] Even Huxley was still agnostic about
evolution, on grounds of lack of evidence, in the 1850s.[35]

To the modern reader Paley's *Natural Theology* seems essentially a
work of the eighteenth century. He shows no interest in the sort of
problems that worried the nineteenth century. He does not concern
himself with reconciling Genesis and geology; indeed he does not
mention either geology or the biblical account of creation. On the other
hand Huxley was able to claim that he 'proleptically accepted the modern
doctrine of evolution'.[36] He was referring to a paragraph in *Natural
Theology* in which Paley observed that there might be many 'second
causes and many courses of second causes, one behind another,
between what we observe of nature and the Deity'. Paley went on to
say that there must none the less be an intelligent designing author.

> The philosopher beholds with astonishment the production of things
> around him. Unconscious particles of matter take their stations, and
> severally range themselves in an order, so as to become collectively
> plants or animals, i.e., organized bodies, with parts bearing strict
> and evident relation to one another, and to the utility of the whole:
> and it should seem that these particles could not move in any other
> way than as they do; for, they testify not the smallest sign of choice,
> or liberty, or discretion. There may be particular intelligent beings,
> guiding these motions in each case: or they may be the result of
> trains of mechanical dispositions, fixed beforehand by an intelligent
> appointment, and kept in action by a power at the centre. But, in
> either case, there must be intelligence.[37]

This certainly suggests a way in which the old natural theology might
be adapted to take account of the conclusions of Darwin and other
scientists. Huxley, the pugnacious champion of science against the
theologians, considered that evolution was not incompatible with
teleology or with theism.[38] Darwin too called himself a theist in the
sense that he could not conceive how the universe could be the result

of blind chance or necessity, and felt compelled to assume a first cause with a mind in some degree analogous to that of man.[39]

Even if Huxley was right about Paley's 'proleptic' acceptance of evolution, it must be acknowledged that the argument from design as he developed it is in the main obsolete. The modern theist would be more inclined to ground his belief on man's moral and intellectual capacities than on the structure of his body. In this sense natural theology is not dead. Its conclusions may not be as clear and compelling as those which Paley drew from nature seemed to him and his contemporaries. But as Bishop Butler pointed out, with religion as with much else in life man has to be content with less than conclusive evidence.

✳ 8 ✳
Evidences of Christianity

Natural Theology does not of course prove the truth of the Christian religion; indeed it might be thought that if the world of nature showed so clearly the hand of God there was no need of further revelation. The theology of the eighteenth century tended to reduce the importance of revelation by comparison with what could be deduced by reason without further aid. The Deists dispensed with revelation, or if they did not reject it outright made it no more than a duplication of natural religion; for them the light of nature was sufficient guide. On the orthodox side revelation was thought of as confirming natural religion and at the same time adding something to it. As Locke put it: 'Reason is natural revelation, whereby the eternal Father of light and fountain of all knowledge communicates to mankind that portion of truth which he has laid within the reach of their natural faculties; revelation is natural reason enlarged by a new set of discoveries communicated by God immediately, which reason vouches the truth of, by the testimony and proofs it gives that they come from God.'[1] Bishop Butler described Christianity as 'a republication and external institution of natural or essential religion', but added that it also contained 'an account of a dispensation of things not discernible by reason'. Natural religion was the foundation of Christianity but not the whole of it.[2] Paley belongs to this eighteenth-century tradition. He believed that revelation confirmed natural theology and gave it greater certainty; it also added something, the assurance of a future state after death. And that this revelation came from God was proved by the miracles which accompanied it.

The miracles recorded in the New Testament had long formed one of the main grounds for the defence of Christian belief. This defence had, however, been weakened earlier in the eighteenth century. Protestant writers were unwilling to allow the genuineness of miracles alleged by the Roman Church to have occurred in recent times; if these were based on fraud or delusion might not the same be said of those recorded in the Bible? What criterion was to be used to verify a miracle? There were those who denied the truth of all except those of the Gospels. Others attacked even these. Attacks produced defences, notably that of Sherlock, who in his *Trial of the Witnesses* (1729) staged a mock trial in which the Apostles were charged with giving false evidence on the resurrection and were found to be not guilty. The common assumption was that if the witnesses were not reliable they must be either fraudulent impostors or 'enthusiasts', that is, deluded fanatics.

In 1748 appeared Hume's essay on miracles. In this he argued that all depended on a contest between opposite experiences. Miracles were by definition contrary to universal experience, and such experience could only be countered by an opposite proof that was superior. 'No testimony is sufficient to establish a miracle unless the testimony be of such a kind that its falsehood would be more miraculous than the fact which it endeavours to establish: And even in that case there is a mutual destruction of arguments, and the superior only gives us an assurance suitable to that degree of force which remains after deducting the inferior.'[3] The orthodox answer to Hume was in effect that universal experience was irrelevant to a unique event such as the Christian revelation and that in the case of the New Testament miracles the testimony was such that its falsehood was incredible. In 1763 Boswell mentioned Hume's arguments to Johnson.

> Let us consider [said Johnson]; although God has made Nature to operate by certain fixed laws, yet it is not unreasonable to think he may suspend those laws, in order to establish a system highly advantageous to mankind. Now the Christian Religion is a most beneficial system, as it gives us light and certainty where we were before in darkness and doubt. The miracles which prove it are attested by men who had no interest in deceiving us; but who, on the contrary, were told that they should suffer persecution, and did actually lay down their lives in confirmation of the facts they asserted.[4]

Paley argued in much the same way in his *Evidences.*
He first establishes to his satisfaction that it was probable or at least not improbable that there should be a revelation, and since a revelation

could only be made by miracles the same could be said of the miracles alleged to have accompanied it. He then argues that it was not to be expected that these miracles should be repeated so as to become the object of that universal experience to which Hume appealed. If we allow the existence of a God we must allow that he may vary the natural order which he has established and may do so for a particular purpose only. Moreover we must account for the testimony, explain how the account arose if it was not true. When a theorem is proposed to a mathematician he tries it out on a simple case and if the result is false he knows it must be wrong. So Paley tests 'Mr Hume's theorem'.

> If twelve men, whose probity and good sense I had long known, should seriously and circumstantially relate to me an account of a miracle wrought before their eyes, and in which it was impossible that they should be deceived; if the governor of the country, hearing a rumour of this account, should call these men into his presence, and offer them a short proposal, either to confess the imposture, or submit to be tied up to a gibbet; if they should refuse with one voice to acknowledge that there existed any falsehood or imposture in the case; if this threat were communicated to them separately, yet with no different effect; if it was at last executed; if I myself saw them, one after another, consenting to be racked, burnt, or strangled, rather than give up the truth of their account; still, if Mr Hume's rule be my guide, I am not to believe them. Now I undertake to say that there exists not a sceptic in the world who would not believe them, or who would defend such incredulity.[5]

Paley proceeds to show that 'there is satisfactory evidence that many professing to be original witnesses of the Christian miracles, passed their lives in labours, dangers, and sufferings, voluntarily undergone in attestation of the accounts which they delivered, and solely in consequence of their belief of those accounts; and that they also submitted, from the same motive, to new rules of conduct'.[6] He argues first from probability. The existence of Christianity must have been due to the activities of its founder and his associates; these activities must have sprung from conviction. They would inevitably involve danger, since they ran counter to Jewish hopes and wishes and in the Roman world had to face prejudice backed by power. We can assume from the nature of the case that the original teachers of Christianity entered on a new life, and that like all founders of sects they encountered opposition and lived a life of labour and suffering. And all the evidence from both Christian and non-Christian sources confirms that this was the case.

When we consider, first, the prevalency of the religion at this hour; secondly, the only credible account which can be given of its origin, viz. the activity of the founder and his associates; thirdly, the opposition which that activity must naturally have excited; fourthly, the fate of the founder of the religion, attested by heathen writers as well as our own; fifthly, the testimony of the same writers to the sufferings of Christians, either contemporary with, or immediately succeeding, the original settlers of the institution; sixthly, predictions of the sufferings of his followers ascribed to the founder of the religion, which ascription alone proves, either that such predictions were delivered and fulfilled, or that the writers of Christ's life were induced by the event to attribute such predictions to him; seventhly, letters now in our possession, written by some of the principal agents in the transaction, referring expressly to extreme labours, dangers, and sufferings, sustained by themselves and their companions; lastly, a history, purporting to be written by a fellow traveller of one of the new teachers, and by its unsophisticated correspondency with letters of that person still extant, proving itself to be written by someone well acquainted with the subject of the narrative, which history contains accounts of travels, persecutions and martyrdoms, answering to what the former reasons lead us to expect; when we lay together these considerations ... there cannot much doubt remain upon our minds, but that a number of persons at that time appeared in the world, publicly advancing an extraordinary story, and for the sake of propagating the belief of that story, voluntarily incurring great personal dangers, traversing seas and kingdoms, exerting great industry, and sustaining great extremities of ill usage and persecution.[7]

Paley follows what was the accepted view in his day, that the Gospels according to Matthew and John were the work of the apostles whose names they bear and consequently of eyewitnesses of the events and that Matthew was the earliest of the Gospels. He is prepared to admit that Mark derived his material from Matthew; as for the material common to Matthew and Luke but not in Mark he considers it by no means improbable that they used 'minutes of some of Christ's discourses, as well as brief memoirs of some passages of his life' which had been previously committed to writing, in fact the source to which nineteenth-century scholarship gave the name of Q.[8] He supposes, reasonably enough, that in the early days of Christianity the apostles, occupied with preaching and travelling, did not think of writing for the information of the public or of posterity. But as time went on accounts would get abroad 'of the extraordinary things that had been passing, written with different degrees of information and correctness. The extension of the Christian society, which could no longer be instructed by a personal intercourse with the apostles, and the possible circulation of imperfect or erroneous narratives, would soon teach some amongst them the expediency of sending forth authentic memoirs of the life and doctrines of their master. When accounts appeared, authorized by the name, and credit, and situation of the writers, recommended or recognized by the apostles and first preachers of the religion, or found to coincide with what the apostles and first preachers of the religion had taught, other accounts would fall into disuse and neglect; whilst these maintaining their reputation (as, if genuine, they would do) under the test of time, enquiry, and contradiction, might be expected to make their way into the hands of Christians of all countries of the world.'[9]

Paley proceeds to give at some length the evidence for the authenticity of the New Testament writings. This had been collected and set out by Nathaniel Lardner, a Nonconformist divine, whose *Credibility of the Gospel History* in seventeen volumes appeared between 1727 and 1757. Paley acknowledged his debt to Lardner; he selected from and arranged the material Lardner had accumulated, and did so with his usual skill and lucidity. The material showed that the evidence for authenticity was not merely as strong as but stronger than that accepted in the case of classical authors.[10] Even supposing that we did not know who wrote the four Gospels, the fact that they were received as authentic accounts of the events on which the Christian religion rested and that they confirm one another and are confirmed by the rest of the New Testament would be sufficient to prove that they give us the story on which the apostles acted. That being so the religion must be true: 'These men could not be deceivers. By only not bearing testimony, they might have avoided all their sufferings, and have lived quietly. Would men in such circumstances pretend to have seen what they never saw; assert facts which they had no knowledge of; go about lying, to teach virtue; and, though not only convinced of Christ's being an impostor, but having seen the success of his imposture in his crucifixion, yet persist in carrying it on; and so persist, as to bring upon themselves for nothing, and with a full knowledge of the consequence, enmity and hatred, danger and death?'[11]

Having proved his first proposition Paley passes to his second: 'That there is NOT satisfactory evidence, that persons pretending to be original witnesses of any other similar miracles, have acted in the same manner, in attestation of the accounts which they delivered, and solely in consequence of their belief in the truth of those accounts.' If the miracles of the New Testament are to be accepted, why should we not accept other recorded miracles? Paley's criterion is that implied in his proposition. If there was any analogy to the story of the rise of Christianity, if any other religious leaders had like the apostles based their ministry on miracles performed within their knowledge and undergone labours and sufferings on that account, Paley would, he claims, have believed those miracles. In fact those of the New Testament are unique. Others were told long after the event, or at a distance from the scene of occurrence, or were based on transient rumours. They are not like those of the New Testament confirmed by cumulative evidence and by particularity; some are happenings of no great significance whose alleged occurrence can be explained by the love of the marvellous, others are believed without examination because they confirm established opinions. Again, a distinction should be made between different kinds of miracles. There are visions which can be explained as delusions; there are 'tentative' miracles, where out of a number of attempts only some succeed. In some cases the occurrence can be explained as non-miraculous; in others stories may have been exaggerated in the telling. Some of the New Testament miracles, Paley admits, may come within these categories, but there are many that do not, and the great variety of those attributed to Christ strengthens the credibility of Christianity.[12]

Traditional apologetic based itself not only on miracles but also on the fulfilment of prophecy. Paley does not make much of the latter; he treats it only briefly as one of the 'auxiliary evidences'.[13] He writes at greater length on the moral teaching of the Gospels. Here, as we have already seen, there is a certain discrepancy between his belief that the purpose of Christ's mission was to confirm by new sanctions what could be discovered by the light of nature and the view which he took over from Soame Jenyns that there were new and unique features in his teaching. For the purpose of his argument, however, this is of little moment. The point he makes is that the excellence of Christ's teaching can only be ascribed to its supernatural origin. Jesus was, in external appearance, a Jewish peasant: 'He had no master to instruct or prompt him. He had read no books, but the works of Moses and the prophets. He had visited no polished cities. He had received no lessons from Socrates or Plato; nothing to form in him a taste or judgement, different from that of the rest of his countrymen, and of persons of the same rank with himself.' His coadjutors were 'a few fishermen upon the lake of Tiberias, persons just as uneducated, and for the purpose of framing rules of morality, as unpromising as himself. Supposing his mission to be real, all this is accounted for; the unsuitableness of the authors to the production, of the characters to the undertaking, no longer surprises us; but without *reality*, it is very difficult to explain, how such a system should proceed from such persons. Christ was not like any other carpenter; the apostles were not like any other fishermen.'[14]

In addition to the positive features of Christ's teaching Paley dwells on the negative, the lack of particularities in his account of the next world, the fact that he did not practise or preach any austerities and engaged in no impassioned devotion, did not sacrifice principles to zeal, showed a sound and moderate judgement with regard to Jewish religion, had none of the sophistry and exclusiveness of the Jews, and did not commit himself to any political position. The picture that emerges is of Christ as seen by the eighteenth century, calm, sober, free from enthusiasm. 'There was no heat in his piety, or in the language in which he expressed it; no vehement or rapturous ejaculations, no violent urgency in his prayers. . . . He never appears to have been worked up into anything like that elation, or that emotion of spirits, which is occasionally observed in most of those, to whom the name of enthusiast can in any degree be applied.'[15]

Among the auxiliary evidences Paley includes the 'undesigned coincidences' between St Paul's epistles and the Acts of the Apostles which confirmed the reliability of both. This had been the subject of his earlier work *Horae Paulinae*. He had intended to summarize its argument in the *Evidences*, but found it impossible to make it intelligible in fewer words than were used in the earlier book. For the same reason no attempt will be made to summarize it here. It is sufficient to say that *Horae Paulinae* is an elegant piece of New Testament criticism and one which was original in its design and execution. Contemporaries observed that Paley ignored the Epistle to the Hebrews, which Lardner, in spite of the strong arguments against Pauline authorship, had regarded as authentic.[16] Paley presumably disagreed with Lardner, and perhaps he should have said so. In the *Evidences* he made use of Hebrews, because 'whatever doubts may have been raised about its author, there can be none concerning the age in which it was written'.[17]

Other auxiliary evidences include the 'candour' of the New Testament writers, the fact that they show no disposition to hide difficulties, the consistency between the various accounts of Christ's manner and methods of teaching, the conformity of facts incidentally mentioned with what is recorded by other writers.[18] A separate chapter is given to the resurrection. There is no doubt at all, Paley points out, that this was asserted by the first teachers of Christianity. If it was not true, either they asserted a falsehood or they were themselves deceived. He has already argued against the possibility of imposture, an explanation which, he now states, has been pretty generally abandoned. There remains that of 'enthusiasm'. This is disproved by the non-production of the body. The only credible explanation for the empty tomb, short of a miraculous one, is that the apostles removed the body; but if they did, we are back at the rejected explanation, that of fraud.[19]

Finally Paley comes to the rapid expansion of Christianity as one of the evidences of its truth. This he supports by an argument which may cause some uneasiness in the reader. He contrasts the success of the apostles with the relative failure of modern missions, particularly in India. 'I lament as much as any man, the little progress which Christianity has made in these countries, and the inconsiderable effect that has followed the labours of its missionaries; but I see in it a strong argument for the divine origin of the religion.' The missionaries in India are men of piety and zeal, and they have the advantage over the apostles in respect of education both absolutely and relatively to those they try to convert. The religion they teach is the same and the religion of those they try to convert is similar to that of the Greco-Roman world. What they lack is those miraculous proofs to which the apostles could appeal.[20] If Paley's argument is accepted it would seem to follow that when the work of the first apostles was completed, none but the slowest progress could be expected in the propagation of Christianity. This is hardly borne out by the facts of history.

Having allowed rapid progress as evidence for the truth of a religion, Paley has to face the problem of Mohammedanism, which on this criterion has as good a claim as Christianity to be a true religion. He admits a certain resemblance between the propagation of the two religions, but argues that the differences between them make any comparison invalid. To quote from his summary:

> What are we comparing? A Galilaean peasant, accompanied by a few fishermen, with a conqueror at the head of his army. We compare Jesus, without force, without power, without support, without one external circumstance of attraction or influence, prevailing against the prejudices, the learning, the hierarchy of his country, against the ancient religious opinions, the pompous religious rites, the philosophy, the wisdom, the authority of the Roman Empire, in the most polished and enlightened period of its existence, with Mahomet making his way amongst Arabs; collecting followers in the midst of conquests and triumphs, in the darkest ages and countries of the world, and when success in arms not only operated by that command of men's wills and persons which attends prosperous undertakings, but was considered as a sure testimony of divine approbation. . . . The success of Mahometanism stands not in the way of this important conclusion, that the propagation of Christianity, in the manner and under the circumstances in which it was propagated, is an *unique* in the history of the species. A Jewish peasant overthrew the religion of the world.[21]

The *Evidences* ends with a consideration of some popular objections to Christianity. First Paley deals with certain questions which involve the degree of authority attaching to the scriptural accounts. He did not consider the doctrine of biblical inspiration essential to a belief in Christianity and did not therefore discuss it;[22] but it is clear that he did not believe in the inerrancy of scripture. He acknowledged the existence of apparent discrepancies between the Gospels, or variations in their account of events, but he found nothing surprising in this. 'The usual character of human testimony is substantial truth under circumstantial variety.' This was shown in the experience of the Law Courts, where apparent or real inconsistencies between different versions did not affect the general reliability of their testimony. It was shown too in written histories. For example Clarendon recorded that the Marquis of Argyle was hanged on the same day as that on which he was condemned; other historians that he was beheaded two days after his condemnation: yet no one doubts that he was executed.[23]

As for the Old Testament, it was a common belief among orthodox Christians, and one which persisted long after Paley's day, that its trustworthiness was guaranteed by the fact that it was accepted by Christ. Paley will have none of this. Admittedly Christ assumed 'the divine origin of the Mosaic institution' and recognized the prophetic character of some of the Hebrew Scriptures. 'But to make Christianity answerable with its life for the circumstantial truth of each separate passage of the Old Testament, the genuineness of every book, the information, fidelity, and judgement of every writer in it, is to bring, I will not say great, but unnecessary difficulties, into the whole system. . . . It is an unwarrantable, as well as unsafe, rule to lay down concerning the Jewish history, what was never laid down concerning any other, that either every particular of it must be true, or the whole false.'[24]

Another objection was that Christianity did not produce universal conviction at the time of its first appearance. Paley advances a number of reasons why this should have been so, among them the fact that, as he shows from several passages in the New Testament, in the time of Jesus miracles did not necessarily produce assent.[25] This might be thought to weaken his main thesis that miracles were necessary to attest and confirm the Christian revelation.

Then there was the objection that a revelation which really came from God would have been so clear to all that by now no one would be ignorant of it and all would accept it; if God had wished to reveal himself to man he would have done so more effectively than this. Here Paley follows Bishop Butler in appealing to the analogy of natural religion. The evidence from nature is also partial and incomplete. Nature shows a system of 'beneficence not optimism'. Rain is beneficial, but it does not always fall where and when it is wanted. It may be that all is for the best, but to judge of this is beyond our powers; all we can judge of is the beneficence of the world of nature, and we should not expect in revelation what we find nowhere else.

If Christianity be regarded as a providential instrument for the melioration of mankind, its progress and diffusion resembles that of other causes, by which human life is improved. The diversity is not greater, nor the advance more slow in religion, than we find it in learning, liberty, government, laws. The Deity hath not touched the order of nature in vain. The Jewish religion produced great and permanent effects: the Christian religion hath done the same. It hath disposed the world to amendment. It hath put things in a train.

Furthermore 'irresistible proof would restrain the voluntary powers too much; would not answer the purpose of trial and probation; would call for no exercise of candour, seriousness, humility, enquiry; no submission of passions, interests, and prejudices, to moral evidence and to probable truth; no habits of reflection; none of that previous desire to learn, and to obey the will of God, which forms perhaps the test of the virtuous principle.' It might well be that the divine purpose is not to produce 'obedience by a force little short of mechanical constraint ... but to treat moral agents agreeably to what they are; which is done, when light and motives are of such kinds, and are imparted in such measures, that the influence of them depends upon the recipients themselves'. Finally Paley suggests that too perfect a revelation of a future state might have distracted men too much from the activities of this world and led to a neglect of business and useful industry. As it is, it is possible to seek salvation through Christianity without interruption of the regular course of human affairs.[26]

Finally there were the allegedly bad effects of Christianity on human happiness. This objection, Paley argues, results from looking for the influence of religion in the wrong place. This influence 'is not to be sought for in the councils of princes, in the debates or resolutions of popular assemblies, in the conduct of governments towards their subjects, and of states and sovereigns towards one another; of conquerors at the head of their armies, and of parties intriguing for power at home (topics, which alone almost occupy the attention, and fill the pages of history); but must be perceived, if perceived at all, in the silent course of private and domestic life. Nay more; even there its influence may not be very obvious to observation. If it check, in some degree, personal dissoluteness, if it beget a general probity in the transaction of business, if it produce soft and humane manners in the mass of the community, and occasional exertions of laborious and expensive benevolence in a few individuals, it is all the effect which can offer itself to external notice. The kingdom of heaven is within us. That which is the substance of the religion, its hopes and consolations, its intermixture with the thoughts by day and by night, the devotion of the heart, the control of appetite, the steady direction of the will to the commands of God, is necessarily invisible. Yet upon these depend the virtue and the happiness of millions. ... Religion operates most upon those of whom history knows the least; upon fathers and mothers in their families, upon men servants and maid servants, upon the orderly tradesman, the quiet villager, the manufacturer at his loom, the husbandman in his fields. Among such its influence collectively may be of inestimable value, yet its effects in the meantime little, upon those who figure upon the stage of the world.' At the same time, slow and indirect though its operation may be, Christianity has affected law and institutions. Paley gives a number of examples of this influence, ending with one which he had very much at heart, the abolition which he hoped would soon be effected of slavery in the West Indies.[27]

Another error made by critics was to attribute to Christianity consequences for which it was not responsible. Intolerant and persecuting laws were only to a small extent attributable to religion, and where persecution was inspired by principle the principle was an erroneous one, not to be deduced from the New Testament. Finally, so long as malevolent passions existed, there would always be occasions for their application.

> Europe itself has known no religious wars for some centuries, yet has hardly ever been without wars. Are the calamities, which at this day afflict it, to be imputed to Christianity? Hath Poland fallen to a Christian crusade? Hath the overthrow in France of civil order and security, been effected by the votaries of our religion, or by its foes? Amongst the awful lessons, which the crimes and miseries of that country afford to mankind, this is one, that, in order to be a persecutor, it is not necessary to be a bigot; that in rage and cruelty, in mischief and destruction, fanaticism itself can be outdone by infidelity.[28]

This if nothing else the modern reader can endorse from the experiences of the present century.

Paley deliberately left doctrinal considerations out of account, and was consequently suspected of Socinianism; as one writer put it, he was accused 'of maintaining a very marked and suspicious reserve on some points, more especially on the important question of our Saviour's divinity'.[29] These suspicions were not unnatural at a time when Unitarianism attracted a number of intellectuals who were unable to accept orthodox doctrine, men like Jebb and Frend and Paley's friend and biographer Meadley. They might be confirmed by references in Paley's sermons to Christ as a 'messenger from God' rather than as God.[30] On the other hand he certainly regarded him as different in nature from other men. In a sermon on Christmas Day he asserted that 'Our Saviour's miraculous birth and still more miraculous life distinguished him from every other person that ever appeared in the world', and went on to speak of his blameless character and his plan of teaching the whole of mankind. 'Surely such a plan was only to be found in the Son of God. . . . If Jesus be the Son of God, then everything which he taught comes to us with the weight and sanction of divine authority.'[31] Elsewhere he spoke of the little knowledge we have of the Trinity; 'but this we seem to know . . . that neither man nor angel bears the same relation to God the Father as that which is attributed to his only begotten Son, our Lord Jesus Christ'.[32] The words are cautious, and might not satisfy the orthodox Trinitarian. No doubt Paley, who based his theology on the New Testament, had little interest in the Christological disputes of the Greek theologians or in the definitions of Nicaea and Chalcedon. For him doctrine was of minor importance; at any rate it could be separated from evidences. 'The truth of Christianity depends upon its leading facts, and upon these alone.'[33]

Since Paley's day the witnesses have been further examined. The Gospels have been subjected to minute scrutiny, with the result that the first and fourth can no longer be confidently accepted as the work of eyewitnesses. There have been scholars who have held that it is impossible to recover the historical Jesus, and that what the Gospels tell us is only what Jesus meant to the early Christians. Yet by and large the evidence remains what it was in Paley's day. The question is, what are we to make of it? Although he declined to enter into doctrinal questions, Paley had his views on the meaning of revelation. For him, as we have seen, its purpose was to confirm the lessons of natural theology and to add to them the assurance of a future state. A modern theologian would be unlikely to think quite in those terms. He might reject the whole idea of natural theology, as Barth does; he might think the assurance of life after death less important than the new significance given by Christianity to life on this earth. He might well be unable to go all the way with Paley on the question of miracles, would make greater allowances for fallibility, would distinguish between different types of miracle, and would lay more stress on the subjective element, the conviction of divine agency left on those who experienced or witnessed its effects than on miracles as objective facts designed to authenticate a revelation. Many of the points that Paley makes in the *Evidences* are still valid, but since his day Christian thought has moved in other directions. It has laid less stress on evidences and more on faith, on religious experience, or on the authority of the Church. Such concepts play little or no part in Paley's thought.

✢ 9 ✢
The Church and the Life of Religion

Paley may justly be called a Low Churchman. His view of the Church was not a high one; for him the best form of church government was that which was most convenient, 'which conduces most to the edification of the people, which pleases them best, and suits with the circumstances and civil constitution of the country'.[1] The founder of Christianity, he observed, had not laid down any precise constitution for the Church; some organization was necessary, but the form it took might vary with different ages and societies. Church establishments were justified as the means of preserving and communicating religious knowledge and they ought to be judged by their effectiveness in achieving this end. 'Every other idea, and every other end that have been mixed up with this, as the making of the Church an engine, or even an *ally* of the state; converting it into the means of strengthening or diffusing influence; or regarding it as a support of regal in opposition to popular forms of government, have served only to debase the institution, and to introduce into it numerous corruptions and abuses.'[2]

From this point of view Paley examines the Church as he knew it. There are, he points out, three essentials to a religious establishment, a professional clergy, a legal provision for their maintenance, and the confining of that provision to a particular sect. The first he justifies on the ground of the teaching function of the Church. Christianity is a historical religion, based on events that took place in the past, recorded in dead languages; to understand the records, to interpret them and to defend the faith based on them, leisure and education are necessary and a kind of education incompatible with any other profession. Then, if there is to be a distinct order of clergy, they must be supported; if their sole means of support were voluntary contributions there was the danger that few would contribute, that preaching would become a kind of begging, and that the preacher would be at the mercy of his congregation. The division of a country into parishes, which Paley regards as an essential part of an establishment, makes it necessary to prefer one sect of Christians above the rest, though his ideal would be a comprehensive national church with only a minimum of tests. He recognizes the right of the sovereign to interfere in religion, provided that his interference conduces by its general tendency to the public happiness. Recognition of this principle would preclude imposing a religion on unwilling subjects; a Popish king, for example, before attempting to force his subjects to adopt his form of Christianity should reflect that his example would be followed by other rulers in favour of a different form. Any form of Christianity, Paley maintains, even the most corrupt, is better, that is more beneficial to mankind, than none at all; but if there is to be a choice between establishing the religion of the ruler and that of the majority of his subjects the advantage lies with the latter course. The contemporary reader would surely have taken this to imply that Roman Catholicism should be established in Ireland, a view which Paley expressed in conversation, though not in print.[3]

He did not, it need hardly be said, express it in the sermon he preached in Dublin at John Law's consecration. He used the occasion to defend the organization of the Church established in England and Ireland, a defence which he published with the somewhat chilling title 'A Distinction of Orders in the Church defended upon Principles of Public Utility'.[4] In the first place, he argues, episcopal government is superior to government by synods and assemblies, since these give rise to disputes and intrigues; 'whatever may be the other benefits of equality, peace is best secured by subordination'. Secondly, the distinctions of the clergy should correspond in some degree with those of lay society, so that each class of society is supplied with clergy of their own rank. Thirdly, respect for the clergy depends on the respect paid to the most elevated members of the profession, the bishops. Finally, 'rich and splendid situations in the Church have been justly regarded as prizes held out to invite persons of good hopes and ingenuous attainments to enter into its service'. If young men of ability did not enter the ministry it would be composed of the refuse of every other profession, and 'the allurement is much greater where opulent shares are reserved to reward the success of a few, than where, by a more equal distribution of the fund, all indeed are competently provided for, but no one can raise even his hopes beyond a penurious mediocrity of subsistence and situation'.

Paley's sermon, we are told, satisfied neither the friends nor the enemies of the Church; the former thought he had conceded too much, the latter that he did not concede enough.[5] It was certainly the case that the Church of his day reflected the class structure of contemporary society, but whether this made it perform its mission more effectively is another matter. Adam Smith thought that the poorly endowed Church of Scotland, where the benefices were nearly equal in value, produced all the good effects which an established church could produce, and that clergymen who enjoyed large revenues inevitably lived in a manner which lost them the respect of the common people.[6] Burke, however, was of the same opinion as Paley and expressed it in more picturesque language. 'Our provident constitution has therefore taken care that those who are to instruct presumptuous ignorance, those who are to be censors over insolent vice, should neither incur their contempt, nor live upon their alms. . . . We have not relegated religion . . . to obscure municipalities or rustic villages. No! we will have her exalt her mitred front in courts and parliaments. We will have her mixed throughout the whole mass of life and blended with all the classes of society.'[7]

That the wealth of the higher clergy was an inducement to enter the ministry, regrettable though it may be, can hardly be denied; otherwise the Church would not have been, as it was in the eighteenth century, an overstocked profession. The emoluments of curates and poorer incumbents were not particularly alluring, but there was always the chance that with luck, aided by due attention to their own interests, they might end up in a comfortable benefice, or even rise higher. Sydney Smith, who was more of a reformer than Paley, shared his views on this point, and at a time when Peel's Ecclesiastical Commission was belatedly attacking the problem of church reform, argued that the prestige of the Church depended on the unequal division of its revenues and that the hope of gaining one of the few prizes in what he frankly called the lottery tempted men into its service.[8]

Paley did not write with the eloquence of Burke or the wit of Sydney Smith. He pitched his defence of the Church in a low key, and defended his observations on the ground that they did not suppose 'any impracticable precision in the reward of merit, or any greater degree of disinterestedness, circumspection and propriety in the bestowing of ecclesiastical preferment, than what actually takes place . . .'. He knew well enough that promotion was the result of influence, family connections, and political considerations more often than of merit. As he put it in his Dublin sermon: 'We will not say, that the race is always to the swift or the prize to the deserving.' Elsewhere he wrote more frankly on the contemporary misuse of the Church's revenues. 'When a man draws upon this fund whose studies and employments bear no relation to the object of it; and who is no further a minister of Christ than as a cockade makes a soldier, it seems a misapplication little better than robbery.' And he asks the question 'whether the impoverishment of the fund by converting the best share of it into *annuities* for the gay and illiterate youth of great families, threatens not to starve and stifle the little clerical merit that is left among us'.[9]

Not only was there great disparity of wealth between the higher and the lower clergy of the eighteenth-century Church; emoluments bore little relation to the amount or the importance of the work to be done. The system could be justified if well-endowed benefices, sinecure prebends and cathedral dignities were treated as the reward for long and laborious service or as a means of promoting religious learning, if in fact endowments officially attached to particular offices were regarded as part of the common fund of the Church to be used for the general benefit of religion. This was how Paley regarded them; if a clergyman, he maintained, was promoting the cause of Christianity, it did not matter from what part of the fund his services to the cause were requited.[10] This was a reasonable view in the circumstances of the day. It implied that non-residence was justified, provided that the parish duty was adequately performed by a curate, and the non-resident incumbent played his part in promoting religion, as Paley himself, who did not reside on all his benefices, could justly claim to have done. He did, however, favour some degree of redistribution of emoluments. Late in his life he drew up a plan for a Bill imposing a tax on non-residence, to be applied to the augmentation of small livings; he took no action, however, and his plan did not get beyond his private papers.[11]

A year before he preached at Law's consecration Paley had addressed what might be called the lower orders of the clergy, in an ordination sermon preached in the chapel of Rose Castle.[12] In a diocese like Carlisle, remote from the universities, many of the ordinands would be 'literates', that is, non-graduates. They were unlikely to rise high in the Church. They would, of course, start as curates, and might long remain in that position, and in many cases perhaps their capacities were not such as to justify any high ambitions. As Paley offered 'reasons for contentment' to the poor labourers, so he pointed out to the newly ordained the advantages enjoyed by curates; they were free from the worries and unpopularity of titheowners, and being on a level with most of their parishioners could gain their confidence in a way that was hardly possible for the higher clergy. He gave some practical advice, which no doubt was based on a thorough familiarity with the life of the clergy and a shrewd understanding of their weak-nesses and temptations. He warns against extravagance, drunkenness, and dissoluteness. He mentions those 'awkward endeavours to lift themselves into importance, which young clergymen not unfrequently fall upon; such as a conceited way of speaking, new airs and gestures, affected manners, a mimicry of the fashions, language and diversions, or even of the follies and vices, of higher life; a hunting after the acquaintance of the great, a cold and distant behaviour towards their former equals, and a contemptuous neglect of their society'. Above all he recommends retirement, the ability to live alone. 'Half of your faults originate from the want of this faculty. It is impatience of solitude which carries you continually from your parishes, your home, and your duty; makes you foremost in every party of pleasure and place of diversion; dissipates your thoughts, distracts your studies, leads you into expense, keeps you in distress, puts you out of humour with your profession, causes you to place yourselves at the head of some low company, or to fasten yourselves as despicable retainers to the houses and societies of the rich.' He touches on something which was much in the minds of the eighteenth-century clergy, the pursuit of preferment. Preferment, he says, is not essential to happiness, but even if it were more important than it is the best rule is to do one's duty contentedly and let things run their course. 'Be assured, that for once that preferment is forfeited by modesty, it is ten times lost by intrusion and importunity.'

On another occasion, when he addressed the academic clergy of Cambridge, he spoke of the more subtle dangers and temptations of the clerical profession.[13] He observed that constant familiarity with religious matters tended to result in an insensibility to religious impressions, that the habit of directing arguments to others led to overstating one's case, and that theological learning could result merely in self-satisfaction. The insensibility that came from familiarity was to be counteracted by 'an effort of reflection; by a positive exertion of the mind; by knowing this tendency, and by setting ourselves expressly to resist it'. It might be inevitable that the teacher of religion and morality should consider the effects of his words on others rather than on himself, but it was unnecessary to aggravate the danger by overstatement and exaggeration, the consciousness of which 'corrupts to us the whole value of the conclusion'. 'Its worst effect is seen ... in its so undermining the solidity of our proofs, that our own understandings refuse to rest upon them; in vitiating the integrity of our own judgements; in rendering our minds, as well incapable of estimating the proper strength of moral and religious arguments, as unreasonably suspicious of their truth, and dull and insensible to their impression.' The self-satisfied biblical critic must remember that the Scriptures are not only to be studied but to be acted upon; if the book is of sufficient importance to deserve our study it ought to command our obedience. Paley ends this impressive discourse with those remarks about irregular morals in men of learning which we have quoted in an earlier chapter.

Paley had always held that engagement was the great source of happiness, and he was conscious that the clergyman's life did not afford sufficient engagement to an active man. 'Amongst the clergy of the Church of England many, without doubt, are very much at their ease. The proper return for this privilege, the proper use of this opportunity, is to convert it to beneficial study.'[14] So he recommended the study of the Scriptures, with an interleaved text, and the writing of sermons; 'you find yourself unable', he said to the Carlisle ordinands, 'to furnish a sermon every week; try to compose one every month'.[15] He also recommended the study of natural history. This took one out of doors, provided an interest for walks, and as the basis of natural theology was of particular relevance to religion. Among other subjects a clergyman could suitably occupy himself with botany, with meteorological observations, and with astronomy, 'a proper, I had almost said the most proper of all recreations to a clergyman'. Scientific knowledge would dignify his activities in the fields and in the garden; 'if a clergyman will farm, he should not be a common farmer; if he will garden, he should not be a mere delver—let him philosophize his occupation, let him mix science with his work'.[16]

The chapters on Duties towards God in Paley's *Moral and Political Philosophy* include a discussion of public worship.[17] Worship being a duty to God, public worship is a necessity, since otherwise most of mankind would not worship at all. At the same time the institution has other incidental advantages. It encourages benevolence and it mitigates the inequalities of society. When men join together in prayer and praise to their creator 'it is hardly possible . . . to behold mankind as strangers, competitors, or enemies; or not to regard them as children of the same family, assembled before their common parent, and with some portion of the tenderness which belongs to the most endearing of our domestic relations'. When rich and poor assemble together for the same purpose their thoughts must turn to the natural equality of the human species, and the artificial distinctions of civil life are forgotten. 'If ever the poor man holds up his head it is at church; if ever the rich man views him with respect, it is there: and both will be the better, and the public profited, the oftener they meet in a situation, in which the consciousness of dignity in the one is tempered and mitigated, and the spirit of the other erected and confirmed.' Charles James Fox once pointed out this passage to Samuel Rogers and described it as excellent.[18]

In the same way Paley justifies Sunday observance on grounds of utility.[19] He argues that the sabbatical institutions of the Jews were binding only on them and that while it is a Christian duty to assemble for worship on the first day of the week, to rest from employment for the whole of that day is a purely human institution. It is, however, one that is beneficial. It conduces greatly to the happiness of the labouring classes; it gives all men the opportunity for religious meditation and inquiry; and 'those whose humanity embraces the whole sensitive creation will esteem it no inconsiderable recommendation . . . that it affords a respite to the toil of brutes'.

If public worship is a duty and a beneficial institution, the question arises whether it should follow fixed forms.[20] Paley decides that on the whole the advantage lies with a fixed liturgy, though he has some criticisms to make of the Church of England services. It should be remembered that in his day the morning service consisted of Mattins,

Litany, and Communion or Ante-Communion. Sermons were shorter than they had once been, and the average morning service was only about an hour and a half long,[21] but even so, according to Paley, its length produced in many 'an early and unconquerable dislike'. They seldom came to church, and when they did, they composed themselves 'to a drowsy forgetfulness of the place and duty'. Paley makes some reasonable suggestions for the improvement of a liturgy whose great merits he readily acknowledged; some omissions, abridgements, and rearrangements could be made, the Epistles, Gospels, and Collects might be selected with more regard for unity of subject, and the Psalms and lessons 'either left to the choice of the minister, or better accommodated to the capacity of the audience, and the edification of modern life'.[22] Modern liturgical reformers, official and unofficial, have done much to meet Paley's criticisms. Perhaps they have gone further than he would have wished; the brief and bright services of today would probably have seemed to him sadly lacking in substance.

To dissenters Paley was, as we have seen, well disposed both on principle and in practice. Addressing his Cambridge pupils who were going to enter the ministry he told them to behave and to preach in such a way as to impress both churchmen and dissenters with the unimportance of their differences. 'Above all things abstain from ridicule or reflection upon their persons and teachers; from reproaching them with the conduct of their ancestors or predecessors of the same sect; from idle reports of their absurdities and immoralities; from groundless suspicions of their insincerity; and particularly from charging them with opinions which they disown, or consequences they do not deduce.'[23] As for the Methodists, he respected them for their sincere piety. But he rejected their principal tenets, and when he attended their meetings, as he evidently had done, he came away reflecting how different their manner was from 'the calmness, the sobriety, the good sense, and I may add, the strength and authority, of our Lord's discourses'.[24] He dealt with the doctrine of conversion in a sensible and uncontroversial sermon, in which he argued that it was a mistake to divide men into two classes, the converted and the un-converted; there were great varieties of religious condition and the consciousness of a great change was not necessary to all.[25]

Eighteenth-century clergymen are sometimes thought of as preaching a cold morality devoid of any real religious feeling.

Hark to the churchman: day by day he cries,
'Children of men, be virtuous and be wise;
Seek patience, justice, temp'rance, meekness, truth;
In age be courteous, be sedate in youth.'—
So they advise, and when such things be read,
How can we wonder that their flocks are dead?[26]

These are the words that Crabbe puts in the mouth of the Methodist
preacher, and some of Paley's sermons, in which he treats moral themes
on the same lines as in his *Moral and Political Philosophy*, might give
some colour to such criticism. But he was himself aware of the danger
of setting up, as he puts it, 'a kind of philosophical morality detached
from religion and its influence', and he urged the clergy of Carlisle
to counteract this fashionable tendency by asserting 'the superiority
of a religious principle above any other by which human conduct can
be regulated'.[27] In general his preaching was not without warmth and
religious feeling. Not that he inclined at all to 'enthusiasm'. Nor did
he place any emphasis on the sacrament of Communion; in his only
sermon on the subject he is concerned to allay the scruples of those who
think themselves unworthy to partake, or who are discouraged at not
feeling an elevation of spirit and glow of devotion.[28] He did, however,
lay stress on other aids to a religious life, prayer, meditation, and self-
examination, and he urged the cultivation of a spirit of devotion
which would make participation in worship sincere and heartfelt.[29] He
commended public worship not only on grounds of duty and utility
but also as 'the best and nearest advance which creatures like ourselves
are capable of making towards a homage in any wise adequate to the
glory and dignity of the Being whom we adore'.[30]

More than a hundred of his sermons were printed. Some of them
repeat what he said in his books; some deal with themes common to
all Christian preachers. Those whose publication he himself authorized
may be taken to represent his mature teaching. The first one, placed
first by his special direction, is on Seriousness in Religion, a theme on
which he had already written in the chapter on Reverencing the Deity
in *Moral and Political Philosophy*.[31] One sermon, to the modern
reader not one of his happiest, shows his consciousness of the difficulties presented to the believer by parts of the Old Testament; it is on the
destruction of the Canaanites described in the book of Joshua, an act

which Paley explains as one of exemplary penal justice accounted for by the incorrigible wickedness of the Canaanites and not inconsistent with the divine character.[32] Usually his text is from the New Testament. In one place he sums up practical Christianity in three words: devotion, self-government, and benevolence;[33] and these three, it might be said, are his main themes. He observes that benevolence may be associated with loose private morals, and good behaviour may spring from other motives than religion; but the purest motive of action is the love of God, the devotion which springs from contemplation of his bounty and the practice of prayer.[34] Religion cannot be divorced from morality. In a series of sermons on the efficacy of the death of Christ, a doctrine which he admits can only be partially understood, he makes it clear that the salvation which is procured by Christ's death is only offered on conditions; the necessity remains of living a good life.[35] In another series he argues that the influence of the Spirit is not arbitrary, but is only given to those who are disposed to receive its aid; the doctrine of grace does not take away man's moral liberty, nor should it cause him to disregard active duties. His duty is to pray for spiritual assistance, and to respond to the suggestions of the Spirit; the immediate effects are on the disposition, but outward conduct will follow.[36]

Finally, there is the theme which recurs in his writings, that of another life after death. In his *Moral and Political Philosophy* virtue was defined as the doing good to mankind for the sake of everlasting happiness; in the *Evidences* he had claimed that the assurance of a future life was the primary object of revelation; in *Natural Theology* he had written of life on earth as a state of probation, preparatory to another world. Similar themes are found in the sermons. He acknowledges that we can have no precise knowledge of what life after death will be like. We shall have bodies, but very different from and infinitely superior to our present ones; we shall be conscious of being the same, and it appears that we shall know one another.[37] Our happiness or misery will depend on our actions here. Though the scriptural accounts of punishments for the wicked are expressed in figurative language, the idea which they convey is a reality.[38] 'That we shall come again to a new life; that we shall by some method or other be made happy or be made miserable, in that new state, according to the deeds done in the body . . . is a point affirmed absolutely . . . in almost every page of the New Testament.'[39] The last sermon in the collection is a short and simple one on 'The General Resurrection'.[40] It may not have been the last which Paley composed, but it is fitting to take it as his final message. It shows his abiding concern for human conduct and it illustrates the unadorned eloquence which he had at his command.

His text is 'The hour is coming in which all that are in the grave shall hear his voice, and shall come forth; they that have done good unto the resurrection of life; and they that have done evil unto the resurrection of damnation.' 'This text', he says, 'is the poor man's creed. It is his religion; it is imprinted upon his memory, and upon his heart: it is what the most simple can understand: it is what, when understood and believed, excels all the knowledge and learning in the universe: it is what we are to carry about with us in our thoughts: daily remember and daily reflect upon: remember not only at church, not only in our devotions, or in our set meditations; but in our business, our pleasures, in whatever we intend, plan, or execute, whatever we think about, or whatever we set about.' We have it on the authority of God himself that we shall come again into a new life, and 'it is not the wise, the learned, the great, the honoured, the professor of this or that doctrine, the member of this church or the maintainer of that article of faith' that will be happy in that other world, but 'he that doeth good'. To those who doubt their capacity to do good Paley says:

> You do not sufficiently reflect, what doing good is. You are apt to confine the notion of it to giving to others, and giving liberally. This, no doubt, is right and meritorious; but it is certainly not in every man's power; comparatively speaking, it is indeed in the power of very few. But doing good is of a much more general nature; and is in a greater and less degree practicable by all; for, whenever we make one human creature happier, or better, than he would have been without our help, then we do good; and, when we do this from a proper motive, that is, with a sense and desire of pleasing God by doing it, then we do good in the true sense of the text, and of God's gracious promise. Now let everyone, in particular, reflect, whether, in this sense, he has not some good in his power; some within his own doors, to his family, his children, his kindred; by his labour, his authority, his example, by bringing them up, and keeping them in the way of passing their lives honestly, and quietly, and usefully.

What good more important, more practicable, than this is? Again, something may be done beyond our own household: by acts of tenderness, kindness, of help and compassion to our neighbours. Not a particle of this will be lost. It is all set down in the book of life; and happy are they who have much there! And again, if any of us be really sorry, that we have not so much in our power as we would desire, let us remember this short rule, that since we can do little good, to take care that we do no harm. Let us show our sincerity by our innocence: that, at least, is always in our power.

❖ 10 ❖
Epilogue

Paley was very much a man of the eighteenth century. With his rationalism, his optimism, his clarity, and his lack of subtlety he represented all that the nineteenth century reacted against. His whole approach to religion was rejected by Coleridge when he wrote of 'the prevailing taste for books of Natural Theology, Physico-Theology, Demonstrations of God from Nature, Evidences of Christianity, and the like', and went on to exclaim '*Evidences* of Christianity! I am weary of the word. Make a man feel the *want* of it; rouse him, if you can, to the self-knowledge of his *need* of it; and you may safely trust it to its own evidence.'[1] Coleridge was one of the influential figures in the history of nineteenth-century thought, but it would be easy to exaggerate his influence and to underestimate that which Paley continued to exercise. Labels such as 'eighteenth century' and 'nineteenth century' are to some extent artificial and misleading; there are no clear dividing lines between different phases in the history of thought. To Leslie Stephen, writing seventy years after Paley's death, he belonged to an intellectual world that had passed away, one that had no sense of history and no understanding of evolution. Yet one edition of his complete works was published after Stephen wrote, and several editions of individual works. Those who bought and read them presumably did not regard them as out of date.

One reason for Paley's posthumous fame was the adoption of his works as textbooks, particularly in his own university. This began in his lifetime with his *Moral and Political Philosophy*, a book which won for him, in the words of a contemporary, a distinction 'singularly glorious and, most probably, unparalleled; we mean the circumstance of its chapters being very frequently subjects for disputation, in the schools of one of our Universities, at the same time with the immortal *Principia* of Newton, or with the chapters of the celebrated *Essay* of Locke'.[2] The man responsible for conferring this distinction on Paley was Thomas Jones of Trinity, who served as Moderator in 1786 and 1787 and introduced Paley's work into the examinations.[3] In 1787, only two years after the publication of the book, when Gunning was respondent in the Acts and Opponencies, one of his subjects was Paley on Utility; in subsequent years we hear of themes for disputation taken from Paley on happiness, on promises, on suicide, and on crimes and punishments.[4] Paley was also used in the Tripos; in 1788, on the last day, there was 'an hour's examination in Locke and Paley', that is, the *Essay on the Human Understanding* and *Moral and Political Philosophy*.[5] The Cambridge Calendar of 1802 describes the final paper as one on 'Logic, Moral Philosophy, and points relative to Natural and Revealed Religion' and states that 'the authors chiefly respected are Locke, Paley, Clarke, Butler, etc.';[6] but in practice it was no more than 'Locke and Paley'.[7] Indeed Locke seems to have dropped out, and it is said that at the beginning of the nineteenth century all that was needed for a degree in this part of the examination was a knowledge of the early part of Paley's work.[8]

College teaching was in line with university requirements. Paley was regularly used for moral philosophy lectures and papers were set on him in college examinations.[9] The tutors did not necessarily accept all his views, and felt themselves free to criticize him; this indeed may be accounted one of his merits, for a textbook which does not provoke disagreement does little to stimulate the mind and leaves its exponents with little to say. Edward Pearson in his lectures at Sidney Sussex criticized certain features of Paley's theory and of its practical applications.[10] In 1832 Adam Sedgwick delivered an address in Trinity chapel in which, after acknowledging the delight which he had himself experienced in studying Paley, he went on to reject his theories and to claim that his utilitarianism had nothing to do with Christian ethics.[11] Sedgwick was an influential figure in Cambridge, second only perhaps to Whewell, who also pointed out what he considered the defects of Paley's theory.[12]

Undergraduates were not expected to do more than reproduce Paley's views, to answer such questions as 'Give Paley's definition of Happiness and Virtue' or 'What is Paley's opinion on subscription to Articles of Religion?' They might be asked to 'Give the reasons which Gisborne urges against Paley's Principles of Moral Philosophy',[13] but they were not encouraged to give their own views. When in the examination of 1829 J. M. Kemble boldly called Paley a 'miserable sophist', the examiners were by no means pleased; there was talk of failing him, but the final decision was not to make a martyr of him.[14] Kemble was one of the early 'Apostles', and his opinion of Paley was shared by others of his circle. They had no lack of encouragement from outside the university. Coleridge set out to oppose Paley's morality in his periodical publication *The Friend*; he described his *Principles* as a corrupter and poisoner of all moral sense and dignity and its use at Cambridge as a 'disgrace to the national character'.[15] To De Quincey Paley as a philosopher was 'a jest, the disgrace of the age',[16] and Shelley claimed that he would rather be damned with Plato and Bacon than go to heaven with Paley and Malthus.[17] Hazlitt vented his malevolence on an imaginary figure whom he called Paley, who, he said, 'employed the whole of his life, and his moderate second-hand abilities in tampering with religion, morality and politics,—in trimming between his convenience and his conscience,—in crawling between heaven and earth, and trying to cajole both'.

> His celebrated and popular work on Moral Philosophy [Hazlitt went on] is celebrated and popular for no other reason, than that it is a somewhat ingenious and amusing apology for existing abuses of every description, by which anything is to be got. It is a very elaborate and consolatory elucidation of the text that men should not quarrel with their *bread and butter*. It is not an attempt to show what is right, but to palliate and find out plausible excuses for what is wrong. It is a work without the least value, except as a convenient commonplace book or *vade mecum* for tyro politicians and young divines, to smooth their progress in the Church or the State.[18]

Paley's book retained its place in Cambridge education until the middle of the nineteenth century, but by then it had lost something of its old importance with changes in the examination system. The Acts and Opponencies came to an end in 1839, and before that date the philosophy paper in the Tripos had come to be designed for 'the Poll' only, that is for those who did not aspire to honours.[19] A clear distinction developed between the ordinary and the honours degree and the examination for the former underwent certain modifications; Paley's *Moral Philosophy*, or, from 1846, three books of it, kept its place until 1857, after which it disappeared from the syllabus. Paley's position was also weakened by the establishment of the Moral Sciences Tripos in 1851; philosophy was now the subject of a more thorough and specialized study than hitherto, and it was not to be expected that those who devised the new tripos would be content to accept him as the standard authority. His work was at first among those listed as subjects for study, but was soon abandoned.[20]

The work of Paley that had the longest life in an examination syllabus was the *Evidences*. Paley himself designed it partly to assist 'the religious part of an academical education'.[21] When he wrote, this part of education was confined to college teaching such as he himself had given as tutor of Christ's, but eventually the *Evidences* obtained a place in university studies. In 1822 it was prescribed for the Previous examination, established in that year, and it kept its place in the syllabus for nearly a hundred years. This examination, popularly known as Little-go, was taken by all undergraduates in their second year, and the *Evidences* therefore formed a part of the education of every Cambridge man until the present century, when its position was eroded by the provision of alternative subjects, first Elementary Logic and then Elementary Heat and Chemistry,[22] until it was dropped altogether in 1920.

There were certainly some who profited by the study of his work. Charles Darwin, who was an undergraduate at Paley's college from 1828 to 1831, records that he could have written out the whole of it with perfect correctness, though not in Paley's clear language. 'The logic of this book,' he wrote, 'and as I may add of his *Natural Theology*, gave me as much delight as did Euclid. The careful study of these works . . . was the only part of the Academical Course which, as I have felt and still believe, was of the least use to me in the education of my mind. I did not at that time trouble myself about Paley's premises; and taking these on trust I was charmed and convinced by the long line of argumentation.'[23] On the other hand, according to one writer, many young men viewed Paley with disgust, because he was forced on them;[24] and as time passed those who were alive to new developments of thought would find him intellectually alien. Half a century after Darwin had read Paley with such pleasure and profit another distinguished Christ's man, J. C. Smuts, felt nothing but distaste for him, and he retained his antipathy throughout his life.[25]

Most students probably regarded the *Evidences* simply as something which had to be got up for examination purposes, and for their benefit the task was lightened by the production of summaries, in some cases with specimen examination questions. Analyses, epitomes, and outlines were published and republished in great numbers from 1795, when the earliest appeared, down to the present century. Among these were verse mnemonics. An anonymous author produced *Rhymes for all the Authors quoted by Paley in the first eight Chapters*; A. J. Wilkinson published an *Analysis* with each chapter fully summarized in verse, and C. W. Empson offered *Paley's Verses, by Paley's Ghost.* A. J. Wilkinson plods laboriously through the *Evidences* in feeble doggerel.

> We learn from nature of the case
> The toils the founders had to face.
> The Christian faith is now alive,
> The Founder must have been active.
> What dangers preaching to the Jew!
> And likewise to the Heathen too.

And so on, his invention flagging badly at the conclusion of the first chapter:

> They must *conform* to what they preach,
> Or none will listen to their speech,
> Spend hours in prayer, *et genus hoc*,
> Think what a change at Antioch!

'Paley's Ghost' is briefer, freer, and more lively. He summarizes the introductory chapter as follows:

> A creator consulted the good of mankind,
> And never through ages showed changes of mind.
> One part of creation was found to obey
> With moral obedience superior sway.
> That the last state depends on the first should be known.
> All this knowledge was lost, till from heaven sent down.
> These truths it was likely would now be revealed
> And could clearly by miracles only be sealed.
> Objectors assert that experience shows
>   A miracle cannot be true;
> And that witnesses human may possibly lie
>   Is found by experience too.

But surely the terms are ambiguous both;
And nature may vary, though terribly loth.

Which is more likely, Hume asketh of you,
The testimony false or the miracles true?
Go tell him that twelve men of sense and of wit
May fairly be reckoned the truth to have hit.

When he comes to Chapter II he enlivens his verses with some Victorian facetiousness, which suggests that Paley was by now regarded as something of a joke:

When Rome was nearly burned down in one great conflagration,
Nero was the only man suspected by the nation;
But just to turn the tide, you know, and rouse the people's ire, sir,
He said it was the Christian men who set the town on fire, sir.

The story of this dreadful act does very much excite us,
Especially as recorded by that good old cock Tacitus.
To serve as candlelights the Christians were well greased, he says,
Or forced in skins to fight were worried by wild beasteses.

These feeble products of the academic underworld are perhaps hardly worth reviving, but at least they remind us that there was another side to nineteenth-century Cambridge than that shown in memoirs of Apostles and other intellectuals. There was the Cambridge of the 'Poll men', who needed all the help they could get to surmount the hurdles placed in the path to a degree. Some of them were far from bright. There was one undergraduate who, confusing the opening of the *Evidences* with that of *Natural Theology*, could write no more in his Paley paper than 'If twelve men find a watch'.[26]

R. W. Church, reviewing the state of the Church of England on the eve of the Oxford Movement, distinguished two main parties, the traditional Anglicans, the 'High and Dry' as their critics called them, and the Evangelicals. In addition he noted that at Cambridge Paley still had his disciples, 'or if not disciples, representatives of his masculine but not very profound or reverent way of thinking'.[27] Paley can hardly be said to have founded a school, and it would be difficult to point to any churchman of eminence who could be called his follower. Yet there must have been many clergymen, sound middle-of-the-road men with no great intellectual pretensions, who had studied their Paley as undergraduates and saw no reason to question what they had learned from him. But the important influences in the nineteenth-century Church were to be found elsewhere, in the Evangelicals, the Tractarians and the so-called Broad Churchmen.

To the Evangelicals Paley would seem cold and lacking in spiritual fervour. And others, not necessarily Evangelical, but influenced by the prevailing sentiment of the nineteenth century, would find him unduly worldly. D. S. Wayland, who as one of Paley's editors is presumably to be counted among his admirers, so far from sharing Meadley's indignation at his failure to reach the episcopate, is inclined to be apologetic about the rewards he attained in the Church; and he laments Paley's failure in his Carlisle ordination sermon to stress the necessity for 'fervent prayer for the Divine blessing'.[28] Paley's freedom in conversation and in private correspondence was alien to the spirit of Victorian Christianity. A letter of his survives written to Edward Law in 1785, in which he gives a lively account of a quarrel between John Law's wife and another lady, ending with the words 'Mrs Law, however, keeps up her spirits, but whether my Lord grows weary of the toils of an unfruitful bed or whatever the cause the Lady is become enormously fat and at times not a little cross.' A mid-nineteenth-century owner of the letter has added the comment: 'A most extraordinary letter for a divine to write and clearly showing that he lacked great piety at this date.'[29]

The Tractarians with their scholarship, devotion, and strong churchmanship would have little sympathy with Paley's theological liberalism and his low view of the church. Nothing could be more alien to Tractarian ideas than his defence of episcopacy 'upon principles of public utility'. Gladstone in his Tory-High-Church youth described Paley's views on the church as 'tainted by the original vice of his false ethical principles and by the total absence of any substantive conception of the visible church'.[30] Norman Sykes has remarked on the contrast between Paley's sermon at John Law's consecration and one of Liddon's delivered in 1885 in which he dwelt on the apostolic succession and the necessity of episcopacy to a true branch of the Church. 'There could', he says, 'be no better measure of the gulf severing the Latitudinarian from the Tractarian positions.'[31]

Then there were the liberals or Broad Churchmen, not so much a party as a group of gifted individuals. They had some affinities with Paley. Thomas Arnold's idea of a comprehensive national church links up with the eighteenth-century movement, in which Paley was involved, for the abolition of subscription. Moreover Paley's authority could be invoked to justify some latitude in the interpretation of the Old Testament. We have already quoted his remark that it was unwarrantable to lay down that either every particular of Jewish history must be true or the whole false. H. H. Milman, whose *History of the Jews* was a pioneer work in English in the application of historical criticism to the Old Testament, quoted this passage in justification of his approach,[32] and Charles Kingsley did the same in the preface to his *Gospel of the Pentateuch* (1863). 'Brought up', he wrote, 'like all Cambridge men of the last generation on Paley's *Evidences* I had accepted as a matter of course ... Paley's opinions as to the limits of Biblical Criticism.' Kingsley's preface brought him a letter from F. D. Maurice which shows the attitude of a more subtle thinker. 'I am glad you can speak so respectfully of Paley's *Evidences* ... I have a sneaking regard for him as a good, tough North of England man not spoiled by his cleverness as a lawyer. But I have been fighting against him all my days; I cannot help thinking he has done much to demoralize Cambridge, and to raise up a set of divines who turn out a bag infidel on Sundays to run him down, fixing exactly where he shall run and being exceedingly provoked if he finds any holes and corners which they do not happen to know of.'[33] Maurice must have known that young men afflicted with doubts did not find that Paley answered all their questions. When A. H. Clough was on the point of resigning his fellowship at Oriel on account of his religious difficulties the Provost recommended him to read, among other authorities, the works of Paley. 'I confess,' replied Clough, 'I do not fancy the books which you speak of exactly fit to meet the doubts with which young men are now familiar.' There was a general feeling, he said in a later letter, that miracles were poor proofs. People asked what had history to do with religion. 'External evidence is slighted; but I think the great query is rather as to the *internal* evidence.'[34]

Whatever the affinities between Paley and nineteenth-century Broad Churchmanship there was little real sympathy. The Broad Churchmen moved with the times and Paley's thought belonged to his own day. In the later nineteenth century, according to Leslie Stephen, it was the fashion to speak of Paley with contempt, 'partly because of his utter inability to be obscure'; Broad Churchmen were 'specially given to sneering at poor Paley's mechanical religion and his confusion of morality with expediency'.[35] Stephen himself has much to say in criticism of Paley, but cannot resist a certain nostalgic admiration for one whom he had presumably accepted without question when a Cambridge undergraduate destined for Holy Orders. 'His admirable lucidity and his shrewd sense', he wrote, 'extort our admiration.... We, children of the twilight, are too often unjust to the man who loves the broad daylight and resolutely clears his mind of fog.'[36]

A hundred years have passed since Stephen wrote, and there is no need now for churchmen, practising or lapsed, to take up such attitudes to Paley. He is no longer required reading, no longer an authority to be accepted or rejected. He has passed into history. He has a secure, if minor, place in the history of English thought; in the history of European thought he would hardly appear at all, for he is essentially an English, even a provincial English figure. Yet the reputation he once enjoyed was not wholly undeserved. He brought to philosophy and theology valuable qualities—common sense, clarity, humour, unpretentiousness—which are not always found in those who write on such subjects. J. M. Keynes recognized his merits when he classed him with Locke, Hume, Adam Smith, Bentham, Darwin, and Mill as belonging to a tradition of humane science 'marked by a most noble lucidity, by a prosaic sanity free from sentiment or metaphysic, and by an immense disinterestedness and public spirit'.[37] Paley had another quality, cheerfulness, which perhaps endeared him to Keynes; for Keynes has recorded how when a young man at Cambridge he scandalized his friends by maintaining that there was nothing wrong in being cheerful.[38] Gloom is still fashionable, and there is much in contemporary life to encourage it. It is refreshing to turn to one who without being complacent or blind to the ills of life remained unfailingly cheerful and convinced that 'it is a happy world after all'.

APPENDIX A

Portraits of Paley

The portrait of Paley painted by Romney in 1789–91,[1] formerly in the possession of Lord Ellenborough, is now in the National Portrait Gallery. Paley is represented standing in a landscape with a fishing rod in his right hand, holding the line with his left. A copy by Sir William Beechey, head and shoulders only, is also in the National Portrait Gallery, and another copy by the same artist, also head and shoulders, is in the hall of Christ's College, Cambridge.

According to Meadley a portrait of Paley with John Law was painted about 1769 by 'Vandermyn, a Cambridge artist'[2] (probably Frans Van der Mijn, 1719–83, or another member of the same family). At the time of writing (1810) this was in the possession of John Ord; its present owner is unknown to me. Nor have I been able to trace the caricature by Bunbury of Paley and Richard Watson in the Schools, designed 'to excite the risible faculties of the residents of the university.'[3]

Paley is depicted in stained glass in the oriel window of Christ's hall, in a window in Giggleswick school chapel, and in one in the vestry of St Alfege, Greenwich.

APPENDIX B

Some Descendants of Paley

Paley's eldest son William had a successful career at Cambridge. After taking his degree as third wrangler he became fellow of his college (Pembroke) and was called to the bar, but died in his thirty-seventh year in 1817. The second son, Edmund, his father's biographer, was educated at Oxford and became rector of Easingwold, Yorks. Two of his sons were men of some note, F. A. Paley the classical scholar and E. G. Paley the architect.

Frederick Apthorp Paley (1815—1888) was educated at Shrewsbury and St John's Cambridge, and after taking his degree stayed on for some years taking pupils until 1846 when he joined the Church of Rome. He supported himself as a private tutor outside Cambridge, but returned in 1860 and lived in the town taking pupils. For a few years he was professor at Manning's short-lived 'Catholic University' in Kensington. He published numerous works of learning, including editions of Hesiod, Aeschylus, and Euripides; he was also a keen student of Church architecture, author of a *Manual of Gothic Mouldings* and other such works. Walter Leaf, who went to him for coaching, described him as 'a curious creature with a dry shrivelled skin and, I might add, a shrivelled nature'.[1] He seems to have been as unlike his grandfather in character as in religion, though it might be said that the keen interest Paley showed in the construction of the bridge over the Wear reappeared in another form in F.A.'s study of Gothic mouldings, as it reappeared more obviously in the professional work of his brother E.G.

Edward Graham Paley (1823–1895) was first a pupil, then a partner of E. Sharpe of Lancaster. From 1868 he was in partnership with H. J. Austin. The firm was responsible for numerous buildings in Lancashire and north-east England. The churches of Paley and Austin have been described by Sir Nikolaus Pevsner as 'of the highest European standard of their years'; but according to Pevsner the genius was supplied by Austin rather than Paley.[2] E. G. Paley 'was not only eminent as an architect but was greatly respected for his personal qualities'; he was 'a man of much general culture and great personal charm of manner'.[3]

One other descendant of Paley deserves mention, Mary Paley Marshall, one of the early women students at Cambridge, who married Alfred Marshall the economist, and after his death was well known to Cambridge economists as the presiding genius of the Marshall Library.[4] Her descent from the archdeacon was through her grandmother, Paley's daughter Mary, who married a Paley of the elder branch of the family.

Further particulars of the Paley family can be found in Burke's *Landed Gentry* under Paley, formerly of Langcliffe and Ampton.

Notes

Chapter 1—Early Life

1 T. Brayshaw and R. M. Robinson, *History of the Ancient Parish of Giggleswick* (1932), p. 106. The names of Adam de Paley and Richard de Paley are found in documents connected with Giggleswick church in the thirteenth century.

2 The house was formerly let to the vicars of Langcliffe and is known as the Old Vicarage. The modern farm house is still known as Paley's.

3 E.P., pp. xv–xvi

4 Best, pp. 168–9. Cf. *Recollections of the Table Talk of Samuel Rogers* (1856), p. 120. Best attempts to reproduce Paley's north-country vowel sounds. I have decided to leave these to the imagination of the reader.

5 E.P., p. xvi

6 Ibid., p. xx

7 Ibid., p. xviii

8 Edmund Paley (p. lxviii) says that his father's accent was not particularly provincial, though it might be called rather wanting in refinement. But to southerners it certainly seemed broad Yorkshire.

9 E.P., p. xviii. The day of his birth has not been recorded. He was baptized in Peterborough cathedral on 30 August. The baptismal register, as the Dean of Peterborough has kindly confirmed for me, does not give the date of birth.

10 *Gentleman's Magazine* (1786), pt ii, p. 825. A new school house, which no longer survives, was built in 1787. New school buildings were designed by Paley's grandson, E. G. Paley.

11 M., p. 6

12 Ibid., pp. 8–9

13 E.P., pp. xxv–vi

14 Winstanley, *Unreformed Cambridge* (Cambridge 1935), pp. 202, 373–4

15 J. Peile, *Biographical Register of Christ's College* (Cambridge 1913) II, pp. 264–8. The majority of those admitted in 1758 went into residence in Michaelmas of that year. Paley's year in the sense of those who went up in Michaelmas 1759 was a small one, only five or six.

16 *Quarterly Review* IX (1813), p. 396

17 *Anecdotes of the Life of Richard Watson* (1818) I, pp. 7–9

18 E.P., pp. xxv, xlii

19 M., p. 9

20 R. Watson, *A Collection of Theological Tracts* I (1765), p. viii

21 *Anecdotes of the Life of Richard Watson* I, pp. 7–18; H. Gunning, *Reminiscences of Cambridge* I, p. 33

22 Ibid., p. 17. In 1774 it was said that college teaching involved almost daily construing in Greek and Latin. *Gentleman's Magazine* 44 (1774), pp. 209–11.

23 M., pp. 10–11, 25–8

24 Richard Watson did not leave college for a single day for the first two years and a half of his undergraduate career. *Anecdotes* I, p. 14

25 E. Hughes, *North Country Life in the Eighteenth Century* II (Oxford 1965), p. 305

26 Ibid., p. 301; M., p. 14

27 Gunning, *Reminiscences of Cambridge* I, pp. 44–5

28 M., pp. 11–12

29 As is suggested by R. Schneider, *Wordsworth's Cambridge Education* (Cambridge 1957), p. 155

30 Best, p. 169

31 Ibid., p. 167; Lord Granville Leveson-Gower (Earl Granville), *Private Correspondence* (ed. Countess Granville, 1916) II, p. 314. I have found no other reference to this incident in Paley's career. At one time he was approached with a view to becoming tutor to Lord Camden, but the proposal did not get as far as a definite offer. E.P., p. liv.

32 M., p. 22n

33 E.P., p. xxviii. Meadley also had doubts, and in his second edition relegated the story to a footnote. According to Edmund Paley, Paley supped on bread and cheese at Dockrel's coffee house in Trumpington Street. According to *Public Characters* V (1802–3), p. 97, he supped in Petty Cury.

34 J. Jebb, *Remarks upon the Present Mode of education in the University of Cambridge* (1772) (*Works* II, pp. 286–8), summarized in Wordsworth, *Scholae Academicae* (1877), pp. 33–8; Winstanley, *Unreformed Cambridge*, pp. 43–7

35 *Anecdotes of the Life of Richard Watson* I, pp. 30–2

36 E.P., p. xxx; Best, p. 211

37 Jebb, *Works* II, pp. 290–4; Wordsworth, *Scholae Academicae*, pp. 45–52

38 *Anecdotes of the Life of Richard Watson* I, pp. 30–1

39 See Leslie Stephen, *English Thought in the Eighteenth Century* (1876) I, pp. 407–8

40 *Transactions of Greenwich and Lewisham Antiquarian Society* III, no. 5 (1930), p. 236. (I owe this reference to Mr J. Watson, local history librarian of the Borough of Greenwich.)

41 Best, p. 168

42 E.P., p. xxxiii; M., p. 39

43 Best, p. 168

44 E.P., p. xliii. Edmund Paley denies Meadley's statement (p. 48) that the dispute was about the distribution of money sent by parents for the benefit of assistants.

45 Information from Miss Jane Isaac of the Lichfield Joint Record Office from the Bishop's Register B/A/1/21. Particulars of Paley's ordination are not recorded in the printed sources, and I am grateful to the Librarian of Lambeth Palace, Mr E. G. W. Bill, for supplying me with the date and the ordaining bishop from the records of dispensations granted to Paley to hold benefices in plurality (Vicar-General Act Book XI, ff. 116, 163; XII, ff. 235, 270).

46 Mr J. V. Stacey, verger of St Alfege, Greenwich, informs me that Paley's name first appears in the parish registers on 5 March 1766, and that between then and June 1767 he signed the marriage register forty times.

47 E.P., p. xliii

48 *Gentleman's Magazine* (1809), pt I, p. 103

49 M., pp. 45–6

50 E.P., p. xxxvii

Chapter 2—Cambridge

1 Thomas Warton, *The Progress of Discontent* (1741)

2 Gunning, *Reminiscences of Cambridge* I, pp. 236–7

3 *Universal Magazine* IV (1805), p. 511

4 M., p. 122

5 Crabbe, *The Borough*, Letter xxiv

6 T. Baker, *History of St John's College Cambridge*, ed. J. E. B. Mayor, p. 1073

7 Adam Smith, *Wealth of Nations*, bk. v, ch. I, pt III, art. 3

8 Peile, *Biographical Register of Christ's College* II, pp. 267–8

9 *Quarterly Review* IX (1813), p. 396

10 Boswell, *Life of Johnson* (ed. Hill and Powell) III, p. 416. Cf. R. Warner, *Literary Recollections* (1830) II, p. 206n. 'I . . . venerated the vastness of his knowledge; the inflexibility of his integrity; the manliness of his principles; the candour of his character, and the rare simplicity of his manners and appearance.'

11 *Quarterly Review* IX (1813), p. 389. The writer is believed to have been T. D. Whitaker, antiquary and topographer (H. and H. C. Shine, *The Quarterly Review under Gifford* (Chapel Hill 1949), no. 252). He does not appear to have been one of Paley's close friends, and he may have exaggerated John Law's influence on him. The common belief that Law was responsible for parts of Paley's *Moral and Political Philosophy* was unfounded. E.P., pp. cv–ci

12 See O. Chadwick, *From Bossuet to Newman* (Cambridge 1957), ch. v for Law's ideas about the possibility of progress in theology.

13 Paley's *Short Memoir of the Life of Edmund Law* was originally published in W. Hutchinson's *History and Antiquities of the City of Carlisle* (1796), pp. 54–6. It was reprinted separately in 1800, and is included in Meadley, pp. 355–66.

14 Dedication to *Moral and Political Philosophy*

15 M., pp. 71–2

16 Ibid., pp. 80–2

17 Letter to Harriet Frend, 23 March 1831. For Frend see Frida Knight, *University Rebel* (1971). Frend was admitted to Christ's in December 1775 and went into residence in 1776. In her book Mrs Knight not unnaturally assumed that he did so in the Michaelmas term, but Paley had left Cambridge by then, and she has since ascertained from the Christ's records that he took up residence on 25 May, 1776. He thus overlapped with Paley for about half the summer term. I am grateful to Mrs Knight for clearing up this point, and for letting me see a copy of Frend's letter, the original of which is now in the Cambridge University library.

18 *Universal Magazine* IV (1805), pp. 414–17. The article is attributed to Frend by Leslie Stephen in his article on Paley in *D.N.B.*, and the attribution seems plausible, even though Frend had so short an experience of Paley's teaching.

19 'A.S.' in *Monthly Magazine* III (1797), p. 360, describing the lectures at his college, says that 'he must have been a very stupid fellow who would absent himself [from the lectures on Locke and Moral Philosophy] given by one of the first characters in the university, now a dignitary of the church. Many of his principles in morality I held in the greatest detestation, though I was formerly pleased with his liberality and his familiar mode of instruction'. This must refer to Paley, though no A.S. is found in the Christ's register for the years of Paley's fellowship.

20 The doubts expressed by Edmund Paley (p. xlivn) about his father's having lectured on Locke must be unfounded. A correspondent in *Notes and Queries*, 1st series, 1852, pp. 243, 373, had a MS copy, taken from lecture notes by a pupil, of Paley's lectures on Locke.

21 E.P., pp. liv–v

22 E.P., pp. cclviii–ix

23 Locke, *Reasonableness of Christianity*, preface

24 See Memoir by John Disney prefixed to Jebb's *Works* (3 vols, 1787).

25 At Oxford subscription was required at matriculation.

26 For the subscription controversy see F. Blackburne, *Works*, ed. F. Blackburne (Cambridge 1804), vols I and VII; Jebb, *Works* I, pp. 31–44, 137–222, III, pp. 221–32; *Gentleman's Magazine* 42 (1772), pp. 41, 146, 292, 294; T. Belsham, *Memoirs of Theophilus Lindsey* (1873), pp. 30–8; Winstanley, *Unreformed Cambridge*, pp. 301–16.

27 *Last Journals of Horace Walpole* (1910) I, p. 9

28 Blackburne, *Works* VII, pp. 15–19; *Gentleman's Magazine* 42 (1772), pp. 61–2

29 Jebb, *Works* II, p. 209n

30 For Crawford, see Winstanley, *Unreformed Cambridge*, pp. 218–24.

31 Jebb, *Works* I, p. 208n

32 Ibid., p. 210n

33 Jebb, *Works* I, p. 139–222

34 The terms of subscription were modified in 1865.

35 M., p. 89. Jebb himself does not specifically attribute the remark to Paley; he refers to 'the lamentations of some who, while they continued members

of the established church and apologised for her impositions, have been wont, very feelingly and ingenuously, to declare that they could not afford to keep a conscience'. (*Works* II, p. 126n.)

36 *Bibliotheca Parriana* (1827), p. 672; Field, *Memoirs of . . . Samuel Parr* (1828) I, p. 187n. Field rightly deplores this remark. So does R. Warner, *Literary Recollections* II, pp. 202–8.

37 Parr, *Sequel to the Printed Paper* (1792), p. 52; Field, *Memoirs of Samuel Parr* I, pp. 116–17

38 E.P., p. li. So too Alexander Chalmers regards the remark as one of those witticisms in which no serious meaning is intended. Life of Paley prefixed to *Works* (1821) I, pp. xvii–xviii.

39 *Quarterly Review* II (1809), p. 84.

40 R. Warner, *Literary Recollections* II, p. 204

41 R. Watson, *Miscellaneous Tracts* II (1815), pp. 4, 147

42 M., p. 92; *Quarterly Review* II (1809), p. 88

43 E.P., p. xlixn

44 *Defence of the Considerations, ad fin.*

45 *M. and P.P.*, bk III, pt I, ch. XXII. Paley's lecture notes show that he took the same line in his college teaching. B.M. Add. MSS 12079, ff. 113–14

46 *Memoirs of the Life and Writings of Thomas Percival, M.D.* (1807), pp. cxlvi–viii (quoted M., pp. 369–74)

47 M., p. 141

48 *Memoirs of Life of Gilbert Wakefield* (1804) I, p. 129

49 G. Dyer, *Privileges of the University of Cambridge* (1824) II, p. 108

50 *M. and P.P.*, bk VI, ch. X

51 *Anecdotes of the Life of Richard Watson* I, p. 48

52 Jebb, *Works* I, pp. 47–112; II, pp. 259–84, 313–70; III, pp. 261–77; *Gentleman's Magazine* 43 (1773), pp. 335–6, 618; 44 (1774), pp. 92, 123–4, 161–4, 188; Winstanley, *Unreformed Cambridge*, pp. 318–30

53 Jebb, *Works* II, p. 266

54 Jebb, *Works* II, p. 352

55 Watson described Jebb as 'a very honest and intelligent but unpopular man' (*Anecdotes* I, p. 48).

56 Winstanley, *Early Victorian Cambridge* (1940), pp. 70, 167

57 Jebb, *Works* I, p. 80n

58 Edmund Law had thought the same. At Cambridge, he wrote, 'young men . . . often sacrifice their whole stock of strength and spirits and so entirely devote most of their first four years to what is called *taking a good degree* as to be hardly good for anything else'. Preface to Archbishop King's *On the Origin of Evil* (ed. 1781), pp. xx–i.

59 Best, p. 171

60 M., pp. 99–100

61 Dyer, *Privileges of the University of Cambridge* (1824) II, p. 108

62 *Universal Magazine* IV (1805), p. 511

63　Best, p. 184. Cf. *Table Talk of Samuel Rogers* (ed. 1856), p. 120

64　E.P., p. xlvi; Mary Milner, *Life of Isaac Milner* (1842), p. 9

65　*Public Characters* v (1802–3), p. 103

66　Paley corrected the proofs of his *Miscellanea Analytica*.

67　*Public Characters* v (1802–3), p. 104; Mary Milner, *Life of Isaac Milner*, p. 7

68　*Universal Magazine* iv (1805), p. 417

69　*Public Characters* v (1802–3), p. 102; *Monthly Magazine* xix, pt 1 (1805), p. 609

70　M., pp. 65–6

71　M., p. 87

72　*Universal Magazine* iv (1805), p. 510

73　*Public Characters* v (1802–3), p. 110; cf. *General Biography* vii (1808), p. 588. In *Monthly Magazine* xix, pt 1 (1805), p. 609, the success of Christ's is attributed partly to Shepherd's contacts with the great.

74　The yearly average intake for the five years of Paley's tutorship, 1772–6, was 10.2; for the previous five years 9.2; for the following five years 9.4.

75　E.P., p. lix

76　Information from Mr A. E. Hollaender, keeper of MSS at the Guildhall Library, from Guildhall Library MSS 9535/3, p. 352; 9548, p. 102; 9551, sect. 2, fol. 52v. The ordination took place in the Chapel Royal of St James.

77　*Cambridge University Calendar*, 1801, p. 22; *Oxford University Calendar* (1810), pp. 51–2

78　*Sermons on Public Occasions* iv (v)

Chapter 3—The Diocese of Carlisle

1　*Transactions of Cumberland and Westmorland Antiquarian and Archaeological Society*, N.S. xxvii (1927), p. 196

2　Ibid.

3　E.P., p. lix

4　J. M. Keynes, *Essays in Biography*, p. 108n

5　The episcopal registers (in the County Record Office, Carlisle) show that a curate was licensed to Musgrave in 1776.

6　See E.P., pp. lix–x, correcting Meadley's statement that Paley passed some of the happiest years of his life at Musgrave and while there engaged in an unsuccessful farming venture.

7　E.P., p. lx

8　M., pp. 116–17; E.P., p. cxii. The list of rectors in Appleby church omits Paley's immediate successor, and so implies that he held the living until 1789.

9　Best, p. 207. Those who know Clonfert today will not be surprised at the small numbers of the congregation.

10　R. Mant, *History of the Church of Ireland* (1840) ii, p. 756. Cf. E.P., p. lviiin

11　W. E. H. Lecky, *History of Ireland in the Eighteenth Century* (1913) iii, p. 168

12 Nichols, *Literary Anecdotes* VIII, pp. 395–6

13 R. Warner, *Literary Recollections* II, p. 207n

14 R. Burn, *Ecclesiastical Law* (ed. 1767) I, p. 87

15 *Victoria County History of Cumberland* I (1905), p. 120

16 Charges VII (*Sermons on Public Occasions* IV)

17 There is no village of Addingham. The parish includes the villages of Little Salkeld and Glassonby.

18 W. Hutchinson, *History of Cumberland* (1794) II, p. 577. The church was rebuilt in 1841.

19 M., p. 168

20 E.P., p. cxiii

21 In 1835 (by which time the value of the benefices had nearly doubled) the average income of a living in the diocese was £175 compared with £285 for the rest of England and Wales. Bouch, *Prelates and People of the Lake Counties* (Kendal 1948), p. 381.

22 E.P., p. cxvii

23 From Chapter Act Book, in the Fratry, Carlisle. The Receiver-General kept the accounts of the cathedral estates.

24 E.P., p. cxlix

25 *Short Memoir of Edmund Law*

26 *Public Characters* V (1802–3), p. 171

27 Best, pp. 195–6. Law's view was shared by Bp Percy, who once told Dr Johnson that 'it might be discerned whether or no there was a clergyman resident in a parish by the civil or savage manners of the people'. Boswell, *Life of Johnson*, ed. Hill and Powell, III, p. 437

28 E.P., p. cxvii

29 Carlisle Episcopal Registers. See also Consistory Court Book (in County Record Office, Carlisle).

30 *Sermons on Public Occasions* II (II)

31 E.P., p. cxlix; *The Farington Diary* VIII, p. 180

32 Charges IV

33 *The Farington Diary* VIII, p. 180

34 E.P., p. lxvii

35 E.P., p. cclix. According to Edmund Paley (p. lxxiii) there were only two 'stolen' sermons (by Hoadly) in his collections. But it was pointed out in *Notes and Queries* XI (1855), p. 454, that one of the sermons published as Paley's by his son was taken almost word for word from one by Porteus.

36 M., p. 49; *Quarterly Review* IX (1813), p. 393; E.P., p. lxiii

37 Ibid., p. lxxiii

38 *Quarterly Review* II (1809), p. 77. Samuel Ogden (see p. 11), famous for his sermon *On Prayer*, was Boswell's favourite preacher. 'I should like to read all that Ogden has written', said Johnson. Boswell, *Life of Johnson* (ed. Hill and Powell) III, p. 248. For a modern appreciation of Paley's sermons see D. W. Gundry in *Theology* LV (1952), pp. 172–3.

39 *Gentleman's Magazine* 62, pt 1 (1792), pp. 197–8

40 Hutchinson, *History and Antiquities of the City of Carlisle* (1796), pp. 78–82;
Bouch, *Prelates and People of the Lake Counties*, pp. 345–6

41 E.P., pp. cxv, clii

42 J. B. Nichols, *Illustrations of the Literary History of the Eighteenth Century*
VIII (1858), pp. 266–7

43 Ibid., p. 268

44 E.P., p. cliii

45 *N.T.*, ch. xxvi

46 *M. and P.P.*, bk vi, ch. vi

47 E.P., pp. cxix–xx

48 He had a relation who had made a considerable fortune as a planter in the
West Indies and was thus well aware of conditions in the plantations. E.P.,
p. cxxiii

49 *M. and P.P.*, bk iii, pt ii, ch. iii; T. Clarkson, *History of the Abolition of the
Slave Trade* (1808) I, p. 94

50 Ibid. II, pp. 37–8

51 M., pp. 375–91

52 *Public Characters* v (1802–3), p. 123

53 E.P., p. cxxiv; *Collected Letters of S. T. Coleridge* (ed. E. L. Griggs) I (1956)
p. 48

54 W. Field, *Memoirs of the Life, Writings, and Opinions of the Reverend Samuel
Parr* I, pp. 186–7. Parr afterwards restored Paley to his old position.

55 *Life of William Wilberforce*, by R. I. and S. Wilberforce, (1839) II, pp. 2–3;
Milner, *Life of Isaac Milner*, p. 83

56 *M. and P.P.*, bk v, ch. v

57 E.P., p. lx

58 *M. and P.P.*, bk ii, ch. v

59 E.P., p. lxii

60 Ibid., p. cxlix

61 *Table Talk of Samuel Rogers*, p. 120

62 *M. and P.P.*, bk iii, pt iii, ch. ix

63 *Table Talk of Samuel Rogers*, p. 120n

64 Best, pp. 180–1

65 *N.T.*, ch. xxvi

66 E.P., p. lxi. The second Lord Ellenborough stated that the fishing rod was
inserted at Paley's request and that the portrait was painted for his father.
(*Notes and Queries*, 15 Nov. 1862.) According to Edmund Paley John Law
was responsible for having the portrait painted, though it was not executed
until he had gone to Ireland. The sittings were in 1789; the portrait was
completed in 1791 and was paid for by the first Lord Ellenborough. (T. H.
Ward and W. Roberts, *Romney* (1904) II, p. 116.)

67 E.P., p. lxxxvi

68 This was an expanded version of some notes he had used in his Cambridge teaching. Ibid., pp. lxxx–i, ccxxxii–iii

69 Ibid., pp. lxxx, lxxxiii

70 M., pp. 124–6; E.P., p. cxi

71 Ibid., pp. cxxxi, cxlvi

72 Life prefixed to Chalmers' edition of Paley's Works (1821), p. xxxix. In spite of its lack of immediate success *Horae Paulinae* lasted well; the final edition was in 1888.

73 *M. and P.P.*, bk III, pt I, ch. I. The passage is found in Paley's Cambridge lecture notes (B.M. Add. MSS 12079, f. 43). It was no doubt inspired by his desire (see preface to *M. and P.P.*) to arouse curiosity by clearly indicating the difficulty before giving the solution.

74 E.P., p. ccix

75 Winstanley, *Unreformed Cambridge*, p. 281

76 E.P., p. cxxii

77 *Quarterly Review* IX (1813), p. 394

78 According to Mary Milner, *Life of Isaac Milner*, p. 71, Milner's appointment was largely due to Pretyman. Gunning (*Reminiscences of Cambridge* I, p. 266) attributes the passing over of Paley to Wilberforce's misrepresentations.

79 Milner, *Life of Isaac Milner*, pp. 73–4; E.P., p. clii

80 Milner, *Life of Isaac Milner*, p. 116

81 M., p. 270

82 Changed from 'constables' to 'other magistrates' in later editions.

83 E.P., pp. ccviii–x; Best, pp. 166–7; *Quarterly Review* IX (1813), p. 399; Lord Granville Leveson-Gower (Earl Granville), *Private Correspondence*, 1781–1821 (1916) II, p. 358

84 See in addition to sources referred to in previous note *Monthly Magazine* XIX, pt I (1805), p. 612; *Diary and Correspondence of Charles Abbot, Lord Colchester* (1861) I, p. 474. Lord Colchester mentioned Paley as a possible bishop in 1804.

85 E.P., pp. ccx–i

86 *Later Correspondence of George III*, ed. A. Aspinall, III (Cambridge 1967), no. 2062

87 E.P., pp. ccviii–x

88 E.P., pp. clvi–vii. Edmund Paley dates this letter March 1794, but this must be a year too early. Paley received the offer from Barrington when he was at Cambridge in 1795.

89 E.P., p. cliv

90 The Dalston registers (ed. James Wilson, Dalston 1895) II, p. 285, record the burial of John 'newly born'. The memorial tablet to Paley's first wife on the east wall of Carlisle cathedral also records the death of an infant son Francis.

91 E.P., p. clxxiii

Chapter 4—Last Years

1 E. Mackenzie and M. Ross, *View of the County Palatine of Durham* (1834) I, p. 288

2 E.P., p. clxviii

3 M., p. 189. According to Edmund Paley (p. clxxiv) such remarks were received as good-humoured sportiveness.

4 M., p. 187

5 *M. and P.P.*, bk VI, ch. XI. He advocated commutation of tithes into corn rents.

6 M., p. 191

7 Advertisement to *Sermons on Several Subjects*. He did not want the sermons to be published for sale, but in view of the demand and to prevent un-authorized sale his executors decided to publish.

8 E.P., pp. clxxx–i

9 Charges VIII

10 G. Crabbe, *Life of George Crabbe* (World's Classics edn.), p. 173

11 E.P., p. clxxxv

12 Ibid., pp. clxxxvi–vii, cxc

13 M., pp. 212–14

14 Best, p. 190

15 *Sermons on Public Occasions* VI

16 *N.T.*, Dedication

17 J. S. Harford, *Life of Thomas Burgess* (1840), p. 201

18 Among his visitors was Sir James Mackintosh who 'passed a few days very agreeably in the delightful society of that eminent person'. *Memoirs of the Life of Sir James Mackintosh* (1835) I, p. 170

19 E.P., pp. clxxiv–vi

20 J. Gloag and D. Bridgwater, *A History of Cast Iron in Architecture* (1948), p. 86

21 E.P., p. clxxiv

22 Referring perhaps to the three who had been his patrons, Porteus, Pretyman, and Barrington.

23 E.P., pp. cliv–v

24 Ibid., pp. clxxix–xxx

25 In the dedicatory epistle addressed to the Bishop of Durham Paley says that the work was undertaken 'at your Lordship's recommendation'; but it appears from what he says later that the choice of subject was his own, and it looks as if his patron did no more than encourage him to write something.

26 E.P., p. cxcvi; *N.T.*, ch. VIII, Of the Bones III

27 The subdeanery had an endowment of its own in addition to a fourth share of the cathedral general fund. To it was annexed the prebend of Crackpole St Mary.

28 Best, p. 194

29 E.P., p. cxciv

30 Ibid., p. cxci

31 E.P., p. cxciv

32 Best, p. 182

33 Ibid., pp. 160–1

34 Ibid., p. 162. Cf. p. 164 and *The Farington Diary* VIII, p. 180

35 E.P., p. cxciii

36 Best, p. 201

37 E.P., p. cxciii

38 *N.T.*, ch. XXVI

39 M., p. 197. Perhaps (Dr Frewen Moor suggests to me) a stone in the ureter.

40 J. R. Fenwick, *Sketch of the Professional Life and Character of John Clark, M.D.* (Newcastle 1806), p. 27

41 *N.T.*, ch. XXVI

42 *Quarterly Review* IX (1813), p. 399

Chapter 5—Moral Philosophy

1 E.P., p. lxxxii

2 *M. and P.P.*, preface

3 B.M. Add. MSS 12079. At the end of the volume (p. 200v) is a column of headings in a different order from that of the notes. About half-way down is a stroke with the words 'Ended 2nd [?] May, 1774'. This suggests that the order of his notes may not represent that of his lectures, and that his material was spread over two academic years, which would be a natural way of proceeding as he lectured to the second and third years together. In addition to the lecture notes, Add. MSS 12079 contains (mostly on the verso) a rough draft of his book, continued in Add. MSS 12078.

4 *M. and P.P.*, preface

5 J. M. Keynes, *Essays in Biography* (1932), p. 108n

6 *M. and P.P.*, bk I, chs. I–IV. This is derived from Locke (*Essay on the Human Understanding* II, xxviii, 7). For the law of honour see also *Sermons Doctrinal, Moral, and Miscellaneous* XLVIII.

7 *M. and P.P.*, bk I, ch. V

8 L. Stephen, *English Thought in the Eighteenth Century* (1876) II, p. 122

9 *On Morality and Religion*, prefixed to Law's translation of William King's *Essay on the Origin of Evil*, 5th edn (1781), p. liv

10 J. S. Mill, *Dissertations and Discussions* (1875) I, pp. 435–6

11 *M. and P.P.*, bk II, chs. III–IV

12 L. Stephen, *English Thought in the Eighteenth Century* II, p. 125

13 *N.T.*, ch. XXVI

14 This point is made by a supporter of Paley, L. Wainewright, *A Vindication of Dr Paley's Theory of Morals* (1830), p. 72. Cf. W. Whewell, *Elements of Morality*, 4th edn (1864), p. 600.

15 *M. and P.P.*, bk II, ch. IV

16 Ibid., bk I, ch. IV

17 Ibid., bk II, ch. XI

18 Ibid., bk III, pt I, ch. V. Cf. *Evidences*, pt II, ch. II

19 *M. and P.P.*, bk III, pt II, ch. X

20 Ibid., bk II, ch. V

21 Ibid., bk II, ch. VI

22 Ibid., bk II, ch. VIII

23 Ibid., bk I, ch. VI

24 Ibid.

25 Ibid.

26 See also *Sermons Doctrinal, Moral, and Miscellaneous* XLVI

27 De Quincey, *Works*, ed. Masson, V, p. 120n

28 Seneca, *Epistulae* 80.6; Augustine, *Confessions* VI.6.10

29 Swift, *Irish Tracts and Sermons* (ed. L. Landa, 1948), pp. 190–8

30 *M. and P.P.*, bk III, pt II, ch. V

31 *M. and P.P.*, bk II, ch. IX

32 The story in Gunning, *Reminiscences of Cambridge* I, p. 12, shows that such cases were discussed in the moral philosophy lectures of eighteenth-century Cambridge.

33 *M. and P.P.*, bk III, pt I, ch. II

34 Ibid., IV

35 Ibid.

36 *M. and P.P.*, bk II, ch. XI

37 *M. and P.P.*, bk III, pt I, ch. I

38 *M. and P.P.*, bk III, pt II, ch. II

39 Ibid., ch. III

40 Ibid., ch. V

41 *M. and P.P.*, bk III, pt III, ch. I

42 Ibid., ch. VII

43 Ibid., ch. VII

44 Ibid., ch. II. See also *Sermons Doctrinal, Moral, and Miscellaneous* XLIV and XLV (on Fornication).

45 *M. and P.P.*, bk III, pt III, ch. IX

46 *M. and P.P.*, bk IV, ch. II. See also *Sermons Doctrinal, Moral, and Miscellaneous* XLI

47 *M. and P.P.*, bk IV, ch. III

48 *M. and P.P.*, bk I, ch. VII. See also *Sermons Doctrinal, Moral, and Miscellaneous* XLI

49 Meadley's theory (p. 104) that Paley developed his utilitarian theory after he published these notes is disproved by the manuscript notes of his lectures in the British Museum.

50   *Evidences*, pt II, ch. II

51   *M. and P.P.*, bk III, pt. III, ch. II

52   L. Stephen, *English Thought in the Eighteenth Century* I, p. 416

53   *Sermons Doctrinal, Moral, and Miscellaneous* VII (III); XLII (VI)

Chapter 6—Political Philosophy

1   *M. and P.P.*, preface

2   B.M. Add. MSS 12079, ff. 83f, 148f

3   *M. and P.P.*, bk VI, ch. II

4   Ibid.

5   *M. and P.P.*, bk VI, ch. III

6   Ibid.

7   *M. and P.P.*, bk VI, ch. III

8   Ibid., ch. IV

9   Ibid., ch. VI

10   Ibid., ch. VII

11   Ibid., ch. VIII

12   Ibid., ch. VII

13   Ibid.

14   Ibid.

15   Ibid.

16   Ibid.

17   Ibid. (my italics). These alterations were noted in some letters in the *Gentleman's Magazine* signed 'Padilla'. *Gentleman's Magazine* 57, 2 (1787), p. 582. Padilla was identified with Mrs Jebb in *Gentleman's Magazine* 58, 1 (1788), p. 99, but wrongly. (M., p. 144)

18   *M. and P.P.*, bk VI, ch. XI

19   See L. Radzinowicz, *History of English Criminal Law and its Administration* I (1948), p. 4.

20   *M. and P.P.*, bk VI, ch. VIII

21   L. Radzinowicz, *History of English Criminal Law and its Administration* I, pp. 714–19.

22   Quoted ibid., p. 715

23   Ibid., p. 248

24   *M. and P.P.*, bk VI, ch. IX

25   Ibid. Cf. *Sermons on Particular Subjects* XXX

26   Sir S. Romilly reckoned that in the second half of the eighteenth century from 50 to 75% of those capitally convicted were executed whereas in the early nineteenth century the percentage had fallen to between 10 and 15%. Radzinowicz, op. cit. I, p. 325.

27   *M. and P.P.*, bk VI, ch. IX

28 Ibid.

29 Radzinowicz, *History of English Criminal Law and its Administration* III (1956), pp. 424–5

30 *M. and P.P.*, bk VI, ch. IX

31 Ibid.

32 Radzinowicz, *History of English Criminal Law*, I, p. 506

33 Ibid., p. 259

34 *M. and P.P.*, bk VI, ch. IX

35 Ibid.

36 *M. and P.P.*, bk III, pt I, ch. X

37 *M. and P.P.*, bk VI, ch. V

38 Ibid., ch. X

39 Ibid.

40 Ibid., ch. XI

41 F. Shehab, *Progressive Taxation* (Oxford 1953), p. 39

42 *M. and P.P.*, bk VI, ch. XI

43 Best, p. 186. Pitt did, however, provide for graduation in respect of incomes below £200.

44 Graduated estate duty had been introduced in 1894.

45 J. Bonar, *Malthus and his Work*, 1885, p. 332

46 *Edinburgh Review* 64 (Jan. 1837), p. 483

47 *N.T.*, ch. XXVI

48 Ibid.

Chapter 7—Natural Theology

1 Kant, *Critique of Pure Reason*, bk IV, ch. III, section VI

2 Xenophon, *Memorabilia* 1.4.5–7

3 Cicero, *De Natura Deorum* II.4

4 Ibid., 87, 90

5 Ibid., 15, 87–8

6 Ibid., 133–62

7 Lactantius, *Inst. Div.* 1.5.37, VII.3.6

8 Colin Maclaurin, *An Account of Sir Isaac Newton's Philosophical Discoveries* (1748), ed. 1775, p. 400, quoted by Robert H. Hurlblatt III, *Hume, Newton and the Design Argument* (University of Nebraska 1965), p. 42. (A useful book, if rather crudely unsympathetic to Paley and the design argument.)

9 Hume, *Dialogues concerning Natural Religion* (ed. Kemp Smith, Oxford 1935) pp. 178, 182–3

10 Ibid., pp. 206–7, 281

11 See Leslie Stephen, *English Thought in the Eighteenth Century* (1876) I, p. 409, n. 1, for references to a number of English works where the watch analogy had been used.

12 Hume, *Dialogues concerning Natural Religion* (ed. Kemp Smith), p. 218

13 *N.T.*, ch. XXII. See, however, Charges VI: 'The heavens declare the glory of God to all: but to the astronomer they point it out by proofs and significations most powerful, convincing, and infinitely sublime.'

14 Sturmius, quoted *N.T.*, ch. III

15 Ibid., ch. VI

16 Ibid., ch. VII

17 Ibid., ch. VIII

18 Ibid., ch. X

19 Ibid., ch. X

20 Ibid., ch. XI

21 *Edinburgh Review* I, 1810 (1802–3), p. 191

22 Lucretius V, 199

23 Tucker, *Light of Nature* (ed. 1837), I, pp. 373–4, 356

24 *N.T.*, ch. XXVII

25 Ibid., ch. XXI

26 *N.T.*, ch. XXVI

27 D. Lack, *Evolutionary Theory and Christian Belief* (1957), p. 73

28 *N.T.*, ch. XXVI

29 Ibid.

30 Ibid.

31 *N.T.*, ch. XXIII

32 *N.T.*, ch. XXIII

33 Darwin, *Origin of Species* (World's Classics edn), p. 213

34 *Autobiography of Charles Darwin* (ed. Nora Barlow, 1958), p. 87; *Life and Letters of Charles Darwin* (ed. F. Darwin, 1887) II, p. 219

35 Ibid., p. 188

36 Ibid., p. 202

37 *N.T.*, ch. XXIII

38 *Life and Letters of Charles Darwin* II, p. 202

39 *Autobiography of Charles Darwin*, pp. 92–3. But Darwin later felt less sure of this.

Chapter 8—Evidences of Christianity

1 Locke, *Essay upon the Human Understanding* VI, 19.4

2 Butler, *Analogy of Religion*, pt II, ch. I

3 Hume, *Of Miracles*, pt I

4 Boswell, *Life of Johnson* (ed. Hill and Powell) I, pp. 444–5

5 *Evidences*, Preliminary Considerations. For an earlier version of Paley's argument for miracles see E.P., pp. ccxlviii–ix

6   *Evidences*, pt I, prop. I

7   Ibid., ch. VI

8   Ibid., ch. VIII

9   Ibid.

10 Cf. Bishop Watson's remark 'That Jesus Christ lived, died, rose from the dead and ascended into heaven are facts established by better historical testimony than that Alexander fought Darius, conquered Persia, and passed into India' (*Anecdotes of the Life of Richard Watson* I, p. 412).

11 E.P., pt I, ch. X

12 *Evidences*, pt I, prop. II, ch. I

13 *Evidences*, pt II, ch. I. See also for an earlier version, E.P., pp. ccxliii–vii. On the other hand Paley devoted three sermons (*Sermons on Particular Subjects* XXXVII–IX) to prophecy and in the first emphasized the strength of the proof from prophecy.

14 *Evidences*, pt II, ch. II

15 Ibid.

16 *General Biography* VII (1808), p. 590; *Monthly Review* IV (1791), p. 381; *Life* by Chalmers, prefixed to *Works* (ed. 1821), I, p. xxxiv

17 *Evidences*, pt I, ch. VII

18 Ibid., pt II, chs III, IV, VI. For an earlier version see E.P., p. ccxxxii

19 *Evidences*, pt II, ch. VIII

20 Ibid., ch. IX, section II

21 Ibid., section III

22 Ibid., pt III, ch. VIII

23 Ibid., ch. I

24 *Evidences*, pt III, ch. III

25 Ibid., ch. IV

26 Ibid., ch. VI

27 Ibid., ch. VII

28 Ibid.

29 *Quarterly Review* II (1809), p. 82

30 *Sermons Doctrinal, Moral and Miscellaneous* X (I), XI (II)

31 *Sermons on Particular Subjects* II; cf. ibid., I; *Sermons Doctrinal, Moral, and Miscellaneous* XII (XVIII)

32 *Sermons on Particular Subjects* XXXIII

33 *Evidences*, pt III, ch. VIII

Chapter 9—The Church and the Life of Religion

1   E.P., p. ccliv

2   *M. and P.P.*, bk VI, ch. X. In referring to the Church as an ally of the state Paley no doubt had in mind Warburton's book *The Alliance between Church and State* (1736).

3   H. Best, *Four Years in France* (1826), p. 69; cf. M., p. 198

4   *Sermons on Public Occasions* III (III). The points he made were briefly summarized in *M. and P.P.*, bk VI, ch. X.

5   *Works*, ed. A. Chalmers (1821 ed.) I, p. xxv

6   Adam Smith, *Wealth of Nations*, bk V, ch. I, pt III, art. III

7   Burke, *Reflections on the Revolution in France, Works* (1886) II, p. 375

8   S. Smith, *Letters of Archdeacon Singleton, Works* (1845) III, pp. 155, 197

9   *M. and P.P.*, bk III, pt I, ch. XIV

10 Ibid.

11 E.P., pp. ccxiii–xxi. He proposed that the stipend of the curate, which was then paid by the incumbent, should be deducted from the taxable sum.

12 *Sermons on Public Occasions* II (II)

13 *Sermons on Public Occasions* IV (V)

14 *Sermons on Public Occasions* VI

15 Ibid. II (II)

16 *Charges* VI. Cf. V

17 *M. and P.P.*, bk V, ch. IV

18 *Table Talk of Samuel Rogers*, p. 93

19 *M. and P.P.*, bk V, chs VI–VIII

20 Ibid., ch. V

21 N. Sykes, *Church and State in Eighteenth-Century England* (Cambridge 1934), p. 238

22 *M. and P.P.*, bk V, ch. V. He observes, however, that brevity can be studied too much; men's attention wanders and a certain amount of amplification and repetition is therefore desirable.

23 E.P., pp. clxxxiv, cclx

24 *Evidences*, pt II, ch. II. Cf. E.P., pp. ccliv–vi for his rejection of Methodist doctrines.

25 *Sermons Doctrinal, Moral and Miscellaneous* XX (VII)

26 Crabbe, *The Borough*, Letter IV

27 *Sermons on Public Occasions* IV (IV)

28 *Sermons on Particular Subjects* XI

29 *Sermons Doctrinal, Moral and Miscellaneous* XI (II)

30 *Sermons on Particular Subjects* XII

31 Edmund Paley calls the sermon 'Causes of Levity in Religion' and prints it as X in *Sermons Doctrinal, Moral and Miscellaneous*. See the advertisement to *Sermons on Several Subjects* for Paley's wishes about the placing of the sermon.

32 *Sermons on Particular Subjects* XX (XXIX)

33 *Sermons Doctrinal, Moral and Miscellaneous* VIII (III)

34 Ibid. XII (VIII); XXXVI (XXI)

35 Ibid. XXI–IV (XVIII–XX)

36 Ibid. XXVII–IX (XXIII–V)

37 *Sermons on Particular Subjects* XXVII (V), XXVIII (XXXIV)

38 *Sermons Doctrinal, Moral and Miscellaneous* VII (XXXI)

39 *Sermons on Particular Subjects* XXVIII (XXXIV)

40 Ibid. XXIX (XXXV)

Chapter 10—Epilogue

1   Coleridge, *Aids to Reflection* (ed. 1904), p. 272

2   *Memoirs of Living Authors*, quoted *Gentleman's Magazine* 75, 1 (1805), pp. 585–6

3   *Public Characters* V, 1802–3, p. 243

4   Gunning, *Reminiscences of Cambridge* I, p. 81; J. F. M. Wright, *Alma Mater* (1827) II, p. 36; Wordsworth, *Scholae Academicae*, pp. 42, 373, 376

5   Gunning, *Reminiscences of Cambridge* I, p. 89

6   *Cambridge University Calendar* (1802), p. xxxviii

7   L. Wainewright, *The Literary and Scientific Pursuits . . . in the University of Cambridge* (1815), pp. 60–1; *A Vindication of Dr Paley's Theory of Morals* (1830), p. 2; C. Neville, *A Defence of Paley's Moral Philosophy* (1839), p. 3; H. Sidgwick in *Mind* I (1876), p. 241

8   Pryme, *Autobiographic Recollections* (1870), p. 92

9   Wright, *Alma Mater* I, p. 279

10 See Pearson's *Annotations on the practical Part of Dr Paley's Principles* (Ipswich 1801), p. ix, referring to his earlier *Remarks upon the Theory of Morals . . .* (Ipswich 1800).

11 Sedgwick, *A Discourse on the Studies of the University* (Cambridge 1833), pp. 49–57

12 W. Whewell, *Elements of Morality* (ed. 1864), pp. viii, 599–604

13 These examples are from the *Cambridge University Calendar* (1802), p. xxxi. The first is given as 'Give Paley's definition of Reason, Faith, Happiness and Virtue', but this can hardly be right, since Paley does not define Reason and Faith. The questions set in 1842 are more sophisticated. See *Cambridge University Register and Almanack* (1843), pp. 16–18.

14 T. W. Reid, *Life of Richard Monkton Milnes* (1890) I, p. 60

15 Coleridge, *Collected Works* 4 (1969), pp. 313–14; *Collected Letters of S. T. Coleridge*, ed. E. L. Griggs, III (1959), p. 720, cf. p. 153; Hazlitt, *Works*, ed. P. P. Howe (1930–4) XVII, p. 114

16 De Quincey, *Works*, ed. Masson II, p. 62; cf. p. 76

17 *Claire Clairmont's Journal*, 8 Nov. 1820

18 Hazlitt, *Works* VII, p. 252

19 H. Sidgwick in *Mind* I (1879), p. 241. For a time, however, from 1846, candidates for mathematical honours were required to take the Paley paper (*Cambridge University Calendar* (1842), p. 15).

20 It does not appear in the list in the Calendar for 1853.

21   *Evidences*, Dedication

22   See *Student's Handbook to Cambridge* (1905) and (1917–18). By 1901 Little-go could be taken before entry, and exemption could be obtained through external school examinations.

23   *Autobiography of Charles Darwin* (1958), p. 59

24   *Academic Errors, or Recollections of Youth*, by a Member of the University of Cambridge (1817), pp. 105–6

25   W. K. Hancock, *Smuts, The Fields of Force* (Cambridge 1968), p. 186n

26   C. A. Bristed, *Five Years in an English University* (1852), p. 133

27   R. W. Church, *The Oxford Movement* (1891), p. 14

28   Paley, *Works* (ed. D. S. Wayland, 1825) I, pp. iv, xiv

29   King's College Cambridge, Keynes MS 182

30   W. E. Gladstone, *The State in its Relations with the Church* (2nd edn 1839), p. 14; cf. p. 19

31   N. Sykes, *Church and State in England in the Eighteenth Century*, p. 426

32   Milman, *History of the Jews*, 3rd edn, Appendix

33   *Life of F. D. Maurice* (ed. Frederick Maurice, 1884) II, p. 450

34   *Correspondence of Arthur Hugh Clough* (ed. F. L. Mulhauser, 1957) I, pp. 225–7, 234, 249

35   L. Stephen, *Essays on Freethinking and Plainspeaking* (1873), p. 37; cf. p. 54

36   L. Stephen, *English Thought in the Eighteenth Century* II, p. 408

37   J. M. Keynes, *Essays in Biography* (1933), p. 120

38   J. M. Keynes, *Two Memoirs* (1949), p. 101

Appendix A—Portraits of Paley

1   See ch. III, n. 66

2   M., p. 88

3   *Universal Magazine* III (IV) (1805), p. 289

Appendix B—Some Descendants of Paley

1   W. Leaf, *Some Chapters of Autobiography* (1932), p. 60

2   *The Buildings of England, South Lancashire*, pp. 44–5

3   *The Builder* (29 Jan. 1895), p. 60; cf. p. 69

4   See Mary Marshall, *What I Remember* and Keynes's memoir in the *Economic Journal* LIV, 1944.

Index